Out of Ink

By

Creative Writing Students of
La Quinta High School

La Quinta High School
Westminster, California

Out of Ink

Edited and Compiled by: Amanda LaPera
Senior Copy Editors: Kristy Diep, Derek Nguyen, Kimberly Nguyen
Copy Editors: Nancy Huynh, HongAnh Nguyen
Section Editors: Christine Do, Kelly Ho, Thanh Le, Kelvin Pham, Hien Phan, Daniela Solano, Vivian Tang, April Trinh, Peter Vu
Design Editors: Kelly Ho, April Trinh
Cover Designed by: Kelly Ho, April Trinh
Interior Editors: Hien Phan, Phuong Traceyle, Emily Tran

Published by La Quinta High School Creative Writing Class

Dedicated to those filled with creativity who want to share their unique stories, poems, and plays with the world.

Table of Contents

FIRST DATE
By Nancy Huynh

Sit down on the counter
And enjoy the show.
Fish on a conveyor belt
Authentic from Tokyo.

The California roll
Catches your eye,
But your Japanese date
Would rather die
If you didn't let that catastrophe go.
A tuna roll slides by
And she picks up the plate.
Your decision is made,
But it was too late
The perfect impression waves goodbye.

Pressure swells up,
On her sixth dish
When are you going to tell her
That you actually hate fish?

LIFE BEYOND
By Kristy Diep

Days like this
I look outside the glass
Window and imagine
Imagine a life
Where a woman doesn't have to be
A man's wife
Where the government is not
Deaf and corrupt
Where judgment is taken
Out of the equation
Where love fuels the planet
And we all join together
To give opportunities
Needed for happiness
Even though that life
Looks near and truly dear
We are within the walls
Behind the glass
Looking from beyond.

THIS IS WAR

By Kimberly Nguyen

The pungent smell of blood radiates through the air
Seeping into your pores like snake venom
A heavy weight lies on your chest
Draining you of every painful breath that escapes from your lungs
In the distance the sound of a young child
Crying by the corpse of his dead mother
Begging for her to wake up.
She never does.

This is war.
The devastating pain that comes from
A man's overwhelming desire for power
Leaving all but destruction in his wake.

This is war.
The cries of the hungry, injured and dying
Fall upon ignorant ears
Too busy listening to the money rolling in
To hear the pleas of the people.

This is war.
Where a child sits alone on a
Broken down medical table
Dazed from the bombings that ripped
her family from her just moments ago.
Where a twelve-year-old boy cries over the dead body
Of his younger sibling—
The only family that he had left.

This is our world.
A place where scar-ridden people have hope for a better future—
That may never appear.
Let us put down our weapons, our plans, our pride
And open our eyes—
To the broken world we have created.
It is only then that we can, maybe, rebuild ourselves.

GROUND ZERO
By Derek Nguyen

A TRIO OF TEARDROP-SHAPED gunships broke through the thick cloud cover, their floodlights bathing the grey hills in a blinding amber glow. They continued to descend until they were just above the dead trees lining the crests, revealing a straight road towards a complex of squat, tan buildings. When they were about half a mile away, the gunships stopped in midair and descended onto the road. In unison, all of their back ramps opened up with soft hisses, and soldiers clad in hazmat armor stepped out.

A captain strode out of one gunship and activated her helmet's comlink. "This is Captain Giovanna to Verania High Command. Alpha, Bravo, and Charlie squad are at the site and have a positive visual of the targets, over."

Interference crackled through her speakers as a gruff voice replied, "Roger, Captain Giovanna. Proceed with…the operation as planned. Report…again when your team has found anything of signifi—" The connection died just as a streak of lightning flashed. Rain began to fall right after, turning into a loud downpour.

"Damn it." She turned around to see a tall reptilian alien stride over to her. "Lieutenant Vel'Umbra, have you been able to get a proper scan on the buildings?"

"Negative, Captain. The storm is making it impossible to get clear scans from this far." He adjusted his onyx armor and shivered. "Permission to speak freely, Captain?"

"Permission granted, Vel."

"I don't like this, Myra." His amber eyes narrowed. "The mission briefing stated that communications with this facility was cut off forty-eight hours ago. Yet only now are we sent to deal with it. It seems out of the norm, doesn't it?"

"I'm worried too, Vel, but we've got our orders. Let's get this over with and get the hell out of this place. It's giving me the creeps." She waved up all of the officers and pointed to a couple of them. "Charlie Squad, remain here with the gunships. Try to get a secure connection with High Command, and keep an eye on your scanners. Nothing can get past you. That's an order."

Looking at the others, Myra said, "Alpha and Bravo squad will move into the facility. We scout out what's happening and duck back out ASAP. That means at the first sign of trouble, we bail. No exceptions."

All of the officers nodded and moved to inform their soldiers about Myra's orders. When everything was ready, Alpha and Bravo squad began walking toward the buildings. The hidden sun dipped below the horizon, causing what little light there was to vanish. When Myra switched on the night vision in her helmet, the world became bathed in blurry greens and black.

As the group arrived at the entrance to the complex, they saw that the barbed wire fences surrounding the perimeter were covered in some sort of darkened dried substance.

A sergeant got up and peered at one prominent streak. "My helmet's readings say that it's blood, a mix of human and Veranian blood." He raised his mag rifle and pointed at the guardhouse set into the fence wall. "Maybe it'll have clues that can tell us what happened."

Myra nodded. "Take a look Sergeant Stryker, and see if you can get the gate open. The rest of you, spread out and cover the area." As the troops split, she followed Stryker to the guardhouse. "Weapons free soldier. All of the windows are broken, and there's blood splattered across the walls."

As they inched up to it, Stryker held up a hand, signaling that he had seen something. He inched up and pointed his rifle through the window. He froze and said, "Captain, you've got to see this."

She peered over the window and almost retched. There were two bodies, one human and one Veranian, slumped against opposite walls. Both were wearing heavy riot gear, which was reserved for facility guards in emergency situations. However, the human one had bizarre growths that looked almost like boils emerging from its torso, and a metallic barb jutting out of the throat. "What the hell is this? It's like he's rotting. And what are those growths?"

Stryker clambered into the guardroom and knelt down by the bodies. "The Veranian is still breathing. Help me with this, Captain." Grabbing the alien by the shoulders, he and Myra hoisted him out and laid him on the ground. Stryker waved at the soldiers and said, "We need a medic over here!"

A soldier dashed over and unslung the medical kit he was wearing. While the medic was trying to revive the alien, Myra took a closer look at the dead human. His skin was still colored, yet it had a yellow tinge to it. His right arm had a large gash running down its length, and there appeared to be serrated blades growing out of it.

Vel strode over and peered over Myra. Wincing at the sight, he asked, "What is that monstrosity? It's like a fusion between a corpse and a machine." He glanced at the buildings. "This just keeps getting worse."

There was a groan, and everyone turned to look at the Veranian on the ground. He lifted his head and looked at the soldiers staring at him. "Where am

I?" Looking at the guardhouse, he shot up and began to backpedal. "Dammit, we need get out of this place now! Get out while there's still time!" Just before he could bolt, Vel grabbed him by the arm.

"Hold on a minute. What's the situation here? Why did everything go dark two days ago?" When the Veranian refused to answer, Vel shook him lightly. "What did you see?"

"I don't know much, I swear." He looked around. "I'm just a guard. All I know is that they were testing some sort of bio-weapon here. About two days ago, we went on red-alert, but the comms all shut down. There were these…things everywhere. We were overrun, but I made it to the surface. Some of those creatures followed me, and I had to kill them. I got knocked out by one and woke up to this." The alien struggled in Vel's grasp. "Please, I have to get out of here."

The lieutenant nodded. "All right, we'll get you out." Gesturing to the road, he said, "Walk down there until you see the gunships, and tell the soldiers that you're a survivor. They'll extract you out of here when the operation is complete."

"No, you don't understand. We have to leave now. Before more of those things come up top." When he saw that Vel couldn't be persuaded to leave, the Veranian sighed and walked down the road to the ships. "If you're all set on going inside, watch out for open doors or holes in the floor. And listen for the clicking. If it gets loud, run and don't look back."

Myra walked up to Vel. "Do you suppose he was telling the truth? Or was he just scared out of his mind?"

"Both." Vel peered at the buildings. "Whatever he saw, it was something terrible. I advise that we heed his warning."

"Agreed." She keyed in the C.O. of Charlie Squad and said, "This is Captain Giovanna, we have a Veranian survivor headed your way. He has some information that you might want to listen to. Be advised, he is distraught and jumpy. If Alpha and Bravo squads do not check in within an hour, leave us. Giovanna out." Myra signaled for the two squads to group up again, then clambered into the guardhouse and opened up the gates. After everyone had entered, she closed them and followed the squads into the complex.

The first building in their path, a vehicle bay, appeared untouched apart from a few cargo sleds placed as some sort of barrier. Next was the guards' barracks and armory, which looked like a war zone. Sprayed across the walls were divots and scorch marks, courtesy of human and Veranian weapons. The pavement around the building had sizable cracks and potholes, as if explosives had detonated in those areas. Corpses lay in pools of their own blood around the building, all of them resembling the rotting one in the guardhouse.

15

"Bravo Squad, stay out here and keep an eye out for any activity. Alpha Squad, follow me. We have to get to the surveillance room and figure out what the hell is going on." Myra readied her scattergun and led her squad into the barracks. The interior was an even bigger mess, with broken furniture overturned and brass shell casings carpeting the floor.

"These guards put up one hell of a fight." Stryker glanced at the long shadows. "There's a ton of those corpse-things laying around here. Wait, what's this?" He knelt down by a couple of them and said, "These are wearing uniforms of the Veranian Science Department. So whatever happened here, it affected the scientists too."

"Another thing to add to the growing list of questions I have. Come on, intel says that the surveillance room is up these stairs." Myra motioned for a soldier to take point then followed behind them up the steps. At the top, they could see a large door labeled "Surveillance." It was ajar, and there was a hand sticking out from the corner. She crept forward and stood next to the wall, listening for movement.

Hearing nothing, she rushed into the room, swinging her scattergun in an arc. There were two human guards, sprawled on the floor and shot up beyond recognition. Both were still clutching their empty pistols, and she could see screams etched on the remnants of their faces. Turning to the wall of monitors, she saw that half of them were either shattered or nonfunctional.

"What was that?" Stryker pointed at a screen in the middle.

As Myra followed his finger, she saw a dark shadow flash by on the screen. There was a soft clicking, then a whiplike appendage smashed the camera. "That was in the main laboratory building, in the underground quarantine center. That Veranian said that some of those things followed him up topside. Are there any breaches they could be emerging from?"

He gestured upwards. "Right there, at the topmost screen on the right. That's the elevator shaft on the ground floor to the quarantine floor down below. It looks like the doors were forced open, most likely by those things. But it's still too narrow for them to flood out of."

"We need to inform High Command about this." She activated her comlink again and said, "Charlie Leader, do you read me? Are you able to patch me in to High Command's communications?"

"I sure can boss, give me a second." There was a small burst of static as her comlink was adjusting frequencies.

The gruff voice of the High Command communications officer she had been talking to earlier rose from the static buzz. "Captain Giovanna, what is your status? We have been trying to reestablish contact with your team, but we were only able to reach Charlie Squad up until now."

"A nasty storm prevented us from getting a clear signal." Myra paused and glanced at the screens. "We've discovered something about the science facility…and it's not good. Almost all personnel we've found so far are dead, and some of them are—"

"Disfigured and covered in metal augments." There was an audible sigh from the other end. "This is a code-red situation. Your squads have new orders: prevent the bio-weapons from leaving the facility by any means necessary. High Command will grant your team clearance to everything in the facility, including a complex-wide self-destruct. We'll scramble reinforcements to your position within thirty minutes as a backup measure. Be warned, this was a black ops project, so there's limited intel on the enemy. All relevant files are being sent to you as we speak."

"Noted, High Command. Captain Giovanna out." As the connection ended, a couple of files appeared in her helmet's HUD. Skimming them, she saw that the creatures had started out as synthetic, bulbous organisms carrying nanomachines in them. The goal was to create an efficient nanomachine transporter and dispenser that would inject them into a soldier's neck using a probe to enhance their combat capabilities, but the process was still imperfect. As a result, they had latched onto the test subjects and killed them before controlling their nervous system to move around.

"Damn black ops researchers, these fools dug their own graves." She turned to Stryker and said, "Round up the squad. We've got work to do."

As her squad exited the barracks, Vel dashed over to her. "Captain, we received the orders." He readied his plasma repeater. "My squad is ready to move out."

She nodded. "Let's move then. The gates of hell need to be welded shut. And we're the lucky ones who have the honor of doing so." There was a collective "OORAH," and they headed towards the laboratory building.

"All right, stay sharp. The elevator shaft is right in the middle of the first floor. Bravo Squad, go seal the doors shut. My squad, cover them. Keep an eye out for anything, we don't know if more have managed to escape. If we do this right, nobody goes home in body bags."

Vel kicked the doors of the building open and everyone rushed inside, creating a semicircle as they moved to the elevator shaft. The heavy downpour and the dim yellow emergency lights in the building created an eerie atmosphere, and the shadows followed their every step. Reaching the opening, Myra's squad created a defensive ring around Vel's team.

A Veranian walked up to the doors and pulled them closed. The screeching from them sliding echoed throughout the facility. He then pulled out a welding tool and began sealing the doors. Turning to Vel, he said, "This might take a while."

For a minute there was no sound apart from the hissing of the welding tool and the low humming from the emergency lights. A corporal looked around and asked, "Where are the damn things? It's as if they're hunting us."

"Quiet soldier." Myra stared into the shadows, waiting for the creatures to shuffle into view. Then it began.

At first it was almost undetectable against the heavy downpour. However it began to grow louder over time, a wave of clicks that seemed to originate from nowhere. Just as it seemed to be right under the tiled floor, the clicking vanished.

One of the Veranians walked towards a darkened hallway. "The sounds ended right over there." He stopped about ten feet away from Myra and stomped on the floor. There was a hollow thud. "There's an opening right below!" He began backing away from the spot.

Before he had taken two steps, the tiles cracked and split apart as one of the creatures vaulted itself out of the hole. It pointed its arm at him, and a serrated probe burst out of the wrist and pierced his neck. A stream of orange fluid flowed down the probe and into the wound.

Stryker was the first to shoot, everyone else not far behind. The mixture of bullets and plasma tore the thing apart in a fountain of orange slime and human blood. A metallic tang rose from its body as the nanomachines inside were destroyed.

Myra glanced at the Veranian that had been attacked and gasped. A bulbous sac had covered up the throat wound, and more were growing on the exposed skin. "You're wounded, get over to a medic." She jolted as he snarled at her.

"It's…too late." He shuddered, and his limbs began to shake. "I…can't feel anything…can't think…" His neck snapped aside as a metal appendage jutted out of it. The thing that used to be one of her soldiers turned to her.

"Don't do this. You need to fight back against its control." She took a step back as the infected Veranian lunged at her, its metal probe ready to jab her in the skull. Myra lifted up her scattergun and pulled the trigger. The high-velocity buckshot tore a gaping hole in his torso and sent him staggering backwards into the hole. Before the gun's boom had faded away, the clicking returned to thunderous volume. Dozens of small, bulbous things leaped out of the hole, followed by five infected humans. Myra opened fire and yelled, "Give 'em hell! Let's show them what we're made of!"

18

Chaos reigned as the soldiers let loose on the creatures, tearing dozens of them into shreds of flesh and metal. Brass shell casings began carpeting the floor as more and more of them leaped and dashed at the soldiers. The Veranians fired as well, the whine of their plasma guns mixing with the boom of the human weapons to create a cacophony.

Just as the initial wave appeared to be lagging, Myra heard a series of loud cracks. Glancing behind herself, she saw the floor collapse in two spots, engulfing three of her soldiers. She could hear their screams as they were consumed by the swarms and turned into more of those things.

As they leapt back up, her heart sank as they raised their weapons and opened fire on what used to be their comrades. She fired at them, tearing chunks of flesh off with each boom of the scattergun. One of them shrugged off a direct blast to the chest and raised its mag carbine. Myra pulled the trigger on her gun and cursed as she heard an empty click.

There was a flurry of turquoise light, and its torso exploded in a burst of orange fluid. Vel slammed the butt of his repeater into the head, and its body collapsed into two pieces. "Get down." He pushed Myra down and sprayed a burst at a pod of the small creatures that were leaping at her, popping them all. "The elevator shaft is sealed, but now there are at least three new openings. We don't have enough soldiers to seal them all and hold off the creatures at the same time."

"You're right." She inserted buckshot shells into her scattergun and blasted apart a member of Bravo Squad that had become infected. "If we could get to the security room, we could input the self-destruct code that'll blow these damn things to hell. But we're surrounded, and the room is upstairs."

By now Alpha and Bravo Squad were being pushed back up to the wall. The attacks never ended, when one monster fell, three more took its place. Soon the bullet casings and empty plasma cartridges had grown into piles on the floor, yet the monsters kept attacking. Twelve soldiers remained from the original eighteen who entered, firing with increasing desperation at the monsters.

Stryker was back to back with Myra. "Hey boss, if we go out, let's go out on our own terms." He pulled out a grenade and tossed it to her.

She caught it and nodded. Just as it looked like they would be overrun, she put her fingers on the pin. Then she heard the loud wail of gunship engines, and on cue a hail of bullets and plasma rained down from above.

Stryker whooped and said, "Well I'll be damned. Charlie Squad and the birds decided to come and lend a hand. What timing."

The three gunships had taken positions overlooking the first floor, opening fire on every creature that crawled out of the pits in the floor. Charlie Squad dropped onto the ground and began fighting their way towards the survivors. Its leader made her way to Myra and said, "Looks like you needed a hand. Too bad we couldn't get here sooner. We didn't know how serious the situation was until we heard all of the gunshots."

"Thanks, I don't know how much longer we could've held out for." Myra took a deep breath and said, "Everyone, move upstairs and get towards the security room. When you get there Vel, activate the self-destruct sequence. We're going to blow this place to hell." As the soldiers began to retreat up the stairs, she connected to the pilots' frequency and said, "When I give you the signal, go up to the roof and prepare for a quick extraction." She then stood by the base of the stairs, providing covering fire.

After the last soldier had gotten to the second floor, Myra began backing up, firing her scattergun at the enemy horde. Just as she turned to run the rest of the way up the stairs, she felt something holding her. Looking down, she saw a decaying hand wrapped around her left leg. The infected human pulled her off balance, and she was dragged closer to the writhing mass.

Before she could be speared with a metal probe, a hail of bullets cut down swathes of infected. Getting up, she saw Sergeant Stryker had gone back down to save her. "Not today boss. Get moving." He primed a grenade, and she followed suit. They tossed them then made a dash for the second floor. A couple seconds later the grenades detonated, demolishing the staircase and everything near it.

"Thanks for the save, Stryker." She began to move, but then saw that he was leaning against the wall. "Are you all right? We need to get moving, before those things get up here."

"It's alright, Captain. You should catch up with the others." He glanced down at his torso, where blood was seeping out between his armor plates. "One of them must've nailed me as we ran up the stairs." Stryker took a step forward, then doubled over and winced. "I'll hold them off myself."

"No you're not." Myra put his arm across her shoulders and began helping him walk. "I'm not leaving you. Not when we're this close to completing the mission." Hearing loud clicking, she quickened her pace.

When they were nearing the fork leading to the security room, the first bulbous blobs reached the second floor. Sensing the pair's presence, the creatures began skittering and jumping towards them. Myra cursed and turned to shoot them, then realized that she her scattergun had no more reserve ammunition. Dropping it, she drew her pistol and fired in a series of controlled bursts.

Stryker drew his own sidearm and began firing. "Just keep moving, Captain...I got this covered." He wheezed and coughed up blood. "I can...buy you time."

Now the infected were leaping onto the second floor. Most of them were holding weapons, and they began firing at Myra and Stryker. She gritted her teeth as several bullets whizzed by her head and slammed into the wall behind her. "Dammit, there's too many of them."

Stryker gasped, and he made a small frown. "It looks like…the end of the line for me." He dropped his pistol, and his shaking hand moved toward a cluster of plasma wounds on his chest. As they rounded the corner to take cover, he collapsed onto the ground. "Sorry Captain." His chest heaved once, and his eyes glazed over.

"No, no, no." Myra began to shake him. "Get up, Sergeant. You can't just bail on me like this." There was no response. She put a shaking hand to his eyes and closed them. A lump grew in her throat, and she punched the wall. "Dammit!" Hearing the horde get closer, she reloaded her pistol and said, "Sit tight Stryker, I'll make sure they pay for this."

There was a guttural roar, and she saw a flash of onyx. Vel dashed by, firing his repeater at the horde of infected. Turning back to her, he saw Stryker's body and his eyes lowered. "His death won't be in vain. Go, now. The self-destruct sequence is already counting down; this whole place will be obliterated in three minutes." The survivors of his squad took up defensive positions, covering the others' retreat. "We'll hold them back for you."

Myra looked at Vel blasting his way through the creatures and took a deep breath. Hailing the pilots on the comlink, she said, "Get your birds up to the roof, people are waiting for extraction." She then went over to Vel and began defending the hallway with Bravo Squad. "Don't you dare suggest that you stay behind to buy us time. We can do this without such heroics."

Vel made a faint smile. "You saw right through me, didn't you?"

"I know my soldiers well." She waved for them to begin retreating. "And I know that I can't afford any more deaths under my command." Their coordinated fire tore apart the creatures, and the superheated plasma began igniting the orange fluids in their bodies, creating a blazing inferno from the corpses.

However, the creatures continued to charge into the hail of bullets and plasma bolts. Some fell onto the flames to smother them out, while the rest trampled over them to get clear shots at the rear guard. A hapless Veranian was speared through the head by an infected human's probe, and another was eviscerated by plasma bolts, spraying black blood all over the wall behind him.

Myra fired the last of her pistol rounds into an infected Veranian, then wrested a plasma repeater from one of the dead Bravo Squad members. Eying her helmet's HUD, she said, "Everyone is onboard the gunships. Let's move."

Before she had finished her sentence, she saw one of the infected rise again. It shot its plasma pistol once before being annihilated by plasma fire. As she stared at the lavender bolt flying towards her, a pair of clawed hands shoved her up the stairs.

When Myra's vision cleared, she saw Vel standing above her. His arms were hanging limp by his side, and there was a burning hole in his chest. She shook her head and said, "No, no, no. Not you too…why?"

"Get moving." He took the gun from her and reloaded it. "My fight…ends here." He bared his teeth in a smile. "It was an honor serving under you…Captain." Leaning against the corner of the wall for support, he resumed firing at the horde.

Myra looked at the rest of Bravo Squad, then back to Vel one last time, and nodded. "Godspeed." Fighting back the tears, she waved for the others to run onto the roof. There was one last gunship hovering beside the building. As the others boarded it, she stood in the rain and took one last glance at the stairway. Vel had now slumped down onto the floor, but he was still firing.

Her comlink crackled as Vel spoke. "Go Myra. I'll be fine." He refused to take his gaze away from the enemy. "Go."

She gulped and hopped onto the gunship. As it ascended into the sky, she kept staring at Vel's location, noting the turquoise flashes. They increased in intensity, and then stopped. Moments later, a series of massive explosions rocked all three buildings in the complex. They collapsed in a shower of concrete and metal, leaving only massive piles of rubble and flames as evidence of their existence.

The survivors stared at the destruction in silence for several seconds. One Bravo Squad member then cleared his throat and asked, "Did we do it Captain? Did we win?"

Myra glanced out of the viewports at the raindrops falling. Tears welled up in her eyes, and she clenched her fists. "Yes, we won. And yet somehow, I feel as if I didn't."

WHITE CHOCOLATE MOCHA
By Peter Vu

I want to tell you that I stay up all night thinking about you,
And that you're the first thing I think about when I wake up.
I want to tell you that I've loved you ever since the day we met,
And that I fall more in love with you day after day.
I want to tell you how much I really care about you,
And how much your happiness really means to me.
I want to tell you that all my love poems are about you,
And that every single love song reminds me of you.
I want to tell you that I get butterflies just by hearing your name,
And that I get upset just by hearing the sound of your voice.
I want to tell you how beautiful your smile is,
And how everything hurts whenever I see you.
I want to tell you that I will always wish the best for you,
And that I wish someday you will be in love with me too.

INFIDEL
By April Trinh

i.

    the gold veins that run
    through me ache,
    one-thousand knives
    pushing outward—
    i am made of exit wounds

ii.

    i am overfilled
    with a sickly sweet
    nectar, a honeyed drink
    that i don't dare indulge
    because it was never
    mine to begin with

iii.

    and the only god i ever believed in
    marked me as dead even when
    my fractured heart pounded
    to the beat of war
    at a fragile time of peace

iv.

    but as rainflowers do
    i bloom in all
    of my fractured pieces
    buried in an unrealised dream
    and i begin again

FOREVER AND ALWAYS
By Tony Truong

Rest in peace forever Donna Tran,
I'll never forget the moments that I held your hand,
You died fighting cancer and you were so strong,
Now the only thing left is a simple song,
You may be gone from this Earth but I'll keep you in my heart,
So much left to say, I don't know where to start,
Losing my mind and I'm constantly screaming,
Don't want to believe, I just want to be dreaming,
Wake me up from this nightmare to end this pain,
So much to lose, but nothing to gain,
You were a lover, but more importantly a friend,
Looking forward to the day that I meet you again

Rest Easy in Paradise,
Donna Tran 112700.021018

NULLUS FIDES
By Hien Phan

IN THIS DOMAIN, HIS peers call him the king's greatest servant, the courageous knight of Eden, kindness in human form. They sing praises about his name, how he, the bringer of justice, had saved the kingdom from the first rebellion. Songs echo through the castle halls, worshipping his sworn loyalty to the kingdom. They give him names such as "hero" and "warrior-prince."

He simply prefers to call himself Mikhail.

Ivory doors burst open to welcome him back from the battlefield. Servants rush out to bring him new clothes, wash his steed, and nurse his wounds. With a tired smile, he gently maneuvers past everyone and simply requests a soft bed and a bath. The king would have to celebrate his victory in his absence.

The pillows welcome Mikhail with a warm embrace when he crumples onto the snow-white sheets. Wet, red hair sinks into the plush, like autumn leaves approaching the winter frost. Despite his damp pillow and his aching heart, sleep overtakes him rather quickly.

Only the softest and kindest words accompany Prince Lucien's smile. Mikhail knows this more than anyone; after all, they walk together like two sides of the same coin. Mikhail remembers the mellifluous laughter that echoed in the hallways and how it lifted his spirit higher than any pair of wings could take him. He dreams of that again, of watching Prince Lucien—an angel sent from above—stride through the castle hallways.

'Mikhail,' his prince calls.

Mikhail rushes over. 'Yes, your highness?'

Lucien gives him a stern look, then laughs. 'There's no one around.'

A blink, an apologetic smile. 'Yes, Lucien?'

'May I ask you for a favor?' When he sees the eager nod, he continues. 'Will you stay by my side?'

'I wouldn't think of any other position,' Mikhail stands up a little straighter and puts a hand over his heart.

'Until the end of time?'

'Yes, your highness.'

'Against all odds?'

'I swear it.'

'Good.' Lucien smiles again, so radiant that Mikhail's heart races inside of his chest. 'I'm glad.'

The sun peeks over the horizon, bidding Mikhail good morning as he rubs his eyes and rises from the bed. A pounding headache accompanies him to the mirror, but he ignores it to brush his hair and prepare for the day. A simple routine consisting of one, two, three steps keeps his day in a monotonous flow like a water clock dripping away.

Day in and day out, he picks up messages and handles orders from the king and travels through towns. And every day, he cranes his neck just a little further to see if Prince Lucien is still in his room.

He's not.

Mikhail sighs and turns around the corner, ready to patrol the providence again. "The sun is setting," he muses to himself. It will go away then return in its beautiful aurora, and then the cycle will repeat. An intrusive thought makes his heart ache for Lucien, but he shakes it away. No matter how much he wishes for his sun to rise in the morning again with him, it cannot happen, so he tries to block out any more of those thoughts by focusing on the task at hand.

Except everywhere he goes, he can almost see Prince Lucien's cape around the corner.

"You've left too much behind," Mikhail murmurs as he walks to the front gate.

Mikhail kneels before his prince. 'You called, Lucien?'

The prince paces around in his room, hands behind his back, then turns to Mikhail. 'The current king is no longer fit to rule.'

'Wh—what are you saying? Lucien, that's—'

'I have a proposal.' He cuts him off with a quick glance. 'On another day, I shall march into the ivory gates and declare this kingdom as mine, for I am the better ruler. I can serve my people with more kindness and more compassion, more justice and more love.'

Mikhail bites his lip, bracing for the next line.

'Will you join me?'

Hesitance. Something, someone, anyone, he begs, please wake him up from this nightmare. The treason stated here is only out of jest, a cruel jocular test of his loyalty. Lucien is not serious with him, right? Right?

And Mikhail, from the otherworldly perspective of a dream, watches himself struggle with the loyalty to his prince or the loyalty to his kingdom. He can only hold his breath and stand frozen with the knowledge of what is to come.

'I'm sorry,' he hears himself say. 'I must serve my kingdom first and foremost.'

Lucien turns around. Mikhail catches a glimpse of his flickering eyes, his shattering heart. 'Very well. You are dismissed.'

Mikhail strokes his horse's mane as she nibbles at the carrots from his hand. His mind wanders a little, though the phantom pains of his scars reel him back in. Footsteps also alert him, forcing his stance to stiffen and still.

"I'm proud of you, Mikhail." King Deithe pulls his cape back to keep it from dragging on the ground.

Mikhail bows. "I only did what was right. Loyalty to the kingdom comes first."

The king takes one look at his knight and, with a sigh, murmurs, "I know, but it doesn't stop us from"—his eyes flicker to the horse—"hurting. Being hurt. His betrayal wounded us all."

Mikhail doesn't meet his eyes.

"Prince Lucien was a fool to turn against me like that. I only hope you do not follow in his path, for there is no one like me. My kindness is boundless; I am slow to anger, yet Lucien still turned on me. You are the righteous one. Never forget that."

"Yes, your majesty."

After the king leaves, footsteps fade away; Mikhail leans on his horse and buries his face into her mane. She whinnies softly, as if she's a part of the zephyr brushing past his hair. He's sworn his loyalty to this kingdom, and to this kingdom he shall remain, for this was the path he chose and the one he will stay on. He repeats it over and over as a ritual to quell the burning ache in his heart, yet uncertainty shakes him when he asks a quick question—who is like the king? He smiles bitterly to himself, for there is no answer to the question.

Then his heart flutters like a trapped bird, and once again he stiffly returns to the ivory gates. There is no answer, he repeats. There is no answer. There is none. So why is there still doubt lingering in his chest?

Suffocating. He's suffocating.

Tears well up at the corners of his eyes, but he shakes them off to preserve his vision for the battlefield. He lets out a cry and charges forward towards the opposing prince. Bloody words sting his lips as he nearly chokes on the death-filled air.

'We could have had it all,' he hears Prince Lucien yell above their clashing weapons. 'This kingdom could have been ours!'

Sometimes he's able to reply.

Mikhail snarls, 'You could have had it all. It was your dream, not mine.'

'What happened to the promise we made to stay together for eternity?' Lucien's blade hides the crack in his voice. Arrows whistle past their ears. Swords collide with armor.

'You had a vow to the kingdom, too.' Mikhail's heart, in all of these dreams, brand a kind of shame that follows him hours after he sleeps and hours after he wakes up. 'You broke your oath, so I will break mine.'

Sorrow, betrayal, pain, oh so much pain *become etched in his irises. That look in the prince's eyes still haunt him. His dream follows a guilt-ridden script that he watches from a distance, unable to intervene.*

Other times his throat catches a lump and refuses to let him scream daggers.

This time it's the latter. He can't breathe.

Gardening turns out to be quite therapeutic for Mikhail's unstable thoughts. Sometimes the caged birds chip and cheep out a song, and he greets them, too. He mostly stands back and admires the iridescent array of petals. The pistils gaze back at him, wordlessly comforting him and asking if he's alright with his choice.

He ignores their sympathy. Instead, he whispers to the flowers and encourages them to grow up tall and healthy. The sunflowers follow only the light above, the one who gives them life, purpose, reason. Water sprinkles onto their leaves, and he watches them with a gentle gaze as they bathe in the sunlight. A part of him envies the plants that could still follow their sun. He sits down for a moment and shifts his attention to the narcissuses bobbing over a pond, partly cursing the prince, then dispels the thoughts and plans his upcoming list of tasks. He looks up and breathes in, feeling the chill of rain sweeping in soon. Ah, perhaps it's a waste to water them so soon.

He wipes his eyes and heads back in.

'Are you going to kill me?' Lucien breathes raggedly and faces Mikhail, who stands over him with a sword at his neck.

Mikhail feels all of his muscles tense. Sometimes he watches from first person as he had witnessed on that day. Other times he runs towards the scene, screaming and begging his past self to not press the blade further.

Either way, he always watches himself whisper something, sheath his sword and walk away, westward back. Lucien is left in the dust, breathing raggedly, covered in tears that are not his own.

He knows in his heart that the prince is still out there, somewhere towards the sunrise horizon opposite of this castle. Mikhail was weak; he could not bear to be the one to end the prince's life, and now he pays the price, for he will never see his light again for as long as he is shackled to this castle.

Each day, week, month that passes by weighs his consciousness and pulls him even further under water until his lungs feel like collapsing from regret. Daily tasks become harder to bear, and his joints creak like worn out doors. Something burns up his energy so quickly that it hurts to move, but he, the knight of Eden, must go on despite the suffering that drags him down. The prince has left an apparition whose laugh twinkles like wind chimes, and oh how Mikhail's heart misses that sweetness! How he wishes to escape into a paradise where only they exist! How he yearns never wake up from such a dream!

Yet the persistent nightmares do not leave him alone. Some days Mikhail relives the battles again—swords clashing, sweat dripping, voices screaming above the dissonance. It orchestrates itself again, and again, and again, until Mikhail can no longer stand it.

Sometimes his dreams take him back to a time before the apocalypse that destroyed the person he called home. When he called his prince by name instead of title, when they laughed together like a pair of joyous bells, when they stood side by side through every battle. These dreams take him to where the candles light their room and stars twinkle outside and the moon gracefully drapes the nightly blanket over them. Ah, but Mikhail knows—despite the numerous sources of light, none match that of Lucien's smile.

His heart aches in these dreams where he watches Lucien's charm blazing through the crowd with a rally that puts thunder and lightning to shame. The prince burns everything in his path to brighten the morale of his army, creating an incandescence that no one else can replicate.

He only realizes how cold the castle walls became when it was too late.

"Your majesty." Mikhail kneels before the king. "I must resign my position."

Shock overcomes the king's senses and leaves him in a spluttering mess.

Mikhail rises and faces upward. "I am no longer your knight."

Like a bird in open space, he turns to leave the ivory gates, and like a risen lion, he pushes aside the guards who bar his exit. With the adrenaline, his pace picks up, running towards the sun like an Icarus with wings outstretched, away from the frantic soldiers trying to catch him and cage him in. Two fingers in his mouth and a whistle-noise calls his steed from her stall. She races with him, running, running, running as he climbs on her back and chases everything and nothing at once. Anywhere outside of these gates, anywhere else away from the thundering soldiers' footsteps behind him.

He recognizes some voices that call for his return, soldiers who had accompanied him and followed in his every footstep; only now, he crosses a line where they could not follow. Desperation clouds their voices, and hesitation halts their weapons. Mikhail knows that battle all too well—to obey their liege or to allow their loved one to escape.

Mikhail strokes his horse's mane when he stops hearing arrows fly by. The soldiers must not have been able to catch up.

He guides his horse through towns that he maps like the back of his hand, and once he rushes past the edge of Eden, he stops to gather his thoughts and allow his steed to rest. Sunset bids him goodnight as he turns to take one last look at his kingdom. The sunlight glare makes it look like an angel guarding the entrance with a blazing sword. As Mikhail rests, he forms a brief speech in his mind; he knows his sins are too grave to be forgiven, but perhaps if he may relieve his mind from guilt by the sword, then perhaps he can finally be free. In the distance, he spots a castle on the east horizon.

Hopefully the king won't mind if he pays a visit.

'Mikhail.'
'Yes, your highness—ah, Lucien?'
'Will you stay by my side?'
'Until the end of time. I miss you too much to leave your side any longer.'

Mikhail wills his hands to stop trembling as he approaches another set of castle gates. He leaves his steed near the post and approaches the front guards, who sneer at his dirty clothing once white.

"Where may I find an audience with"—he searches for a fitting title—"His majesty, King Lucien?"

"And who might *you* be to demand something without prior notice? You aren't even dressed in something worthy of his presence." They wrinkle their noses and step back. "This is *the* King Lucien of Hiraeth you're requesting to speak with."

"Relay a message that Mikhail would like to see him."

"Is that you? Why should we do that?"

"His majesty will understand. Please, I wish to see him again."

The guards exchange a look and one rushes in to alert the king. After a few agonizing minutes, a glimpse of a shining crown makes its way towards the gates.

"Who sent you?" King Lucien's voice booms from the doors. "Have you been sent to kill me?"

"No one has sent me but myself." Mikhail feels his heart flutter like a caged bird. "On the contrary, I—" He hesitates. "I've come to ask for my execution."

"What a bold thing to request." Lucien's eyes flicker. "Do you remember your broken oath?"

"Like it was yesterday, your majesty." He kneels down and lays his sword in front of him. "I came here knowing full well that forgiveness may be impossible to ask for, so please, if I may beg for your sword through me—"

"Enough." Lucien waves the guards away and approaches Mikhail. "*I am the king in this domain; you do not give orders.*" He pauses in front of him. "Get up."

Mikhail does as he's told without eye contact.

"Did you come here willingly, not bound by any ties to anyone else?"

"I did."

"If I spare your life, do you promise to serve me and this kingdom until your last breath?"

He hesitates, widening his eyes. "I"—dumbfoundedness keeps his voice from remaining as firm as he would like—"do."

"If I forgive you, do you promise to uphold these laws and take care of our people?"

"I do."

"Kneel," King Lucien commands, and Mikhail does so. Picking up the sword off of the ground, the king taps on his shoulders and kisses the blade. "Since you have accepted your new role, rise and declare your loyalty to me."

Mikhail rises and looks at his king. "I, Mikhail, take this kingdom of Hiraeth"—his heart pounds in his chest—"to be my utmost responsibility. I promise to be faithful, in good times and in bad, in sickness and in health, to love and to honor your name all the days of my life."

Lucien smiles, and suddenly the world brightens from its luminescence. "Welcome, Mikhail of Hiraeth. We have much to discuss." He opens his arms.

And Mikhail rushes into his warm embrace. One laughs, then the other, two voices dancing in the wind like a pair of wedding bells. A vow created, never to be broken for all eternity—only this time it is the kind of vow that no man can separate.

"Your highness," Mikhail blurts, exhilarated. "I—I mean, your majest—"

"Please, just Lucien is fine."

In this domain, Lucien can call him whatever name he would like. Songbird, sparrow, skylark. His retainer, his knight, his beloved. He can whisper sweet words and gentle wishes as well as command him under "my trusted warrior" or "my risen lion," perhaps even "my greatest pride and joy." The king knows that his rose would be alright with any other name.

He simply prefers to call him Mikhail.

TO DEATH, FOR MY HOMELAND
By Edison Sesmas

Our enemy marches forward
Bringing total disorder along our border
They rush from the River Volga
To enslave my homeland: Polska.

Though children and women wave with tears swelling
I depart to the front with young soldiers sweating
Crowds have gathered to bid us farewell
Bless us with Providence as they flee to citadel.

Though a trench is where I dwell
I continue to prepare for a fight to repel
with bayonets attached to the end of each weapon
We shall defeat he who promises Armageddon.

Though blood covers my countenance
And I lack any necessary sustenance
The foe pierces forward through our line
And all but is left of my scarred body is time.

Though a grave death has arranged
My resolve remains unchanged
As my ancestors have done before
To death, for my homeland, I swore.

1999

By Nancy Huynh

THE CITY'S STILLNESS WAS magnified as the golden lights of the historic castle went dark. Built in the 1900s, the castle's lights shone constantly without explanation—there were no electric lines or cables that connected it to any power grid or generator. It was suspected to be a government secret, hidden from the public. Because of this feared conspiracy, the castle doors remained closed and heavily guarded with chains and locks until someone could uncover the mystery of the glowing castle lights.

While walking home from work, Jack counted his dollars and coins over and over again. He had to make sure none were missing, or else he would have to skip lunch again. He felt satisfied and slipped the money back into his pocket. A chill snaked through his body. He looked up to notice the castle's door was open. The chains were gone. He glanced around. There wasn't anyone in sight.

"This can't be *the* castle," Jack said, perplexed by the darkness and abandonment. He paused to check his surroundings and took a few steps forward. An inescapable urge to enter the castle engulfed him. He'd read about numerous people who claimed to investigate the castle, but no results had been published. In fact, Jack didn't remember reading any follow-up articles on the purported investigations.

"I could be rich," Jack whispered, imagining the camera flashes and him speaking on live television and radio shows about how he solved the first mystery of the castle. Jack envisioned a better life after his newfound fame—full of money, admirers, and security. He smiled at the thought.

Jack passed through the towering gates and approached the formidable wooden door. His hands barely touched the handle before he stopped himself.

"What if I get caught?" He took a few steps back away from the castle door. His eyes, however, refused to look away. He thought about the twenty dollars in his pocket and his nearly empty apartment. A sense of loneliness washed over him. *What do I have to lose?* He took a deep breath and, not wanting to move it, squeezed his way through the partially open door.

Using his phone as a flashlight, Jack tiptoed inside the ancient castle and down what seemed like a never-ending hallway, panning the light over the walls that entrapped him. The wall to his left was plastered with large portraits of royalty. The first prominent portrait was from 1990; a hefty king with his wife standing behind him. She held his shoulders tightly and Jack felt like her somber gaze followed him as he moved on to the next frame.

1992—a different, slender king with a smug smile. The gaunt faced woman who stood behind this king looked eerily similar to the woman in the previous portrait, but her hands were placed on the crook of this man's neck. Jack shivered as he noticed the faintest smirk on her face.

The next frame was dated 1994—another king, this time, with an open mouth, as if in the middle of laughing; but the same woman didn't share his joy. Her shadow blended into the background, and if it wasn't for her piercing golden eyes, Jack wouldn't have noticed she was there.

1995—the final picture—a grinning king and the same queen beside him. Jack was fond of the picture, for the queen finally looked as confident as the king.

Jack leaned in closer to examine the portrait, his eyes focused on the object in her hand: a polished, silver knife.

Jack shivered. He walked with quicker strides until he approached the end of the hallway. A cold air brushed against his forearms, and he could've sworn he heard a whisper along with the chilling breeze. He held his phone tightly, panning the light to view his options. *Which way to go?* The pathway to his left led into complete darkness. There was a open door further down the path to his right.

Thump.

Jack's eyes darted between the three hallways, searching for the source of the sound.

Thump. Thump. Thump.

The thumps grew louder and louder, closer and closer, but he didn't know from where. His hands shook; the once steady stream of light became an angry ball of fire. Goosebumps spread over his arms as his light shone on a shadow by the front door.

Jack's mind and body froze. His heart pounded against his chest, and he strained to hear the loud noise again—to see the shadow again, but was met with complete silence and darkness. He shifted his feet back to lean against the wall, taking deep breaths to calm his mind.

"The coffee was strong today." He rubbed his eyes and walked toward the open door.

He squeezed through the narrow door frame, panning his light around the empty room and almost making a complete 180 before it shone on a wooden desk in the corner. His footsteps echoed as he approached the table. Papers and manila folders spread across the surface and the floor. The drawers were open, as if someone had raided through them. Jack propped his phone on a pile of folders so the light shone on the table.

Tyler Seldecky, 1992

Renoir Flint, 1994

Christian Lenn, 1995

Above each caption was a photograph of a beast either surrounded or entrapped by women. Each beast looked nearly human, and Jack saw himself in them. Maybe it was their piercing wide eyes; or their dark, silky hair, that made Jack feel so familiar. He flipped through more photographs of the mysterious creatures, until he found photographs of the women. The pictures had the same title, and the same woman was found in each one. She stood with her arms crossed and head high. The beasts were always at her feet. Her frazzled hair stuck out of her glistening crown, her fangs stuck out of her lips, and her fiery eyes bore into Jack's soul.

Vanity and greed feeds the queen.

He shut his eyes, but the woman's face flashed through his mind.

"Arrgh!" he flung his hands across the table, sending a tornado of papers, and his phone, to the floor.

Jack's deep breaths filled and echoed throughout the dark room as he leaned against the table. He needed to leave. Now.

"It's him." A soft breeze brushed against Jack's ear.

He dropped to the ground, searching for his phone in the dark, but only felt the cold wooden floor and flood of papers.

"It's him."

Jack screamed. "No! Please, no!" His shaking hands swept the ground as he cried out.

A light blinded Jack's vision, and it wasn't from his phone.

Tears and cold sweat dripped down his face as he slowly turned to face the light.

"It's him!" A pale girl screamed, her mouth stretching into a dark hole. Jack struggled to his feet and ran out the door as fast as he could. The narrow hallway seemed even tighter as the girl chased Jack—her deafening screams competing with his own.

"It's him! It's him!" The girl's face stretched more and more the louder she screamed; her hair curled up the faster she ran. Jack's eyes widened in the darkness, searching for an exit—anything to get away from the maniacal girl behind him. The only light in the castle came from the girl's red and green eyes. Jack became dizzy and eventually ran out of breath. His knees buckled, causing his head to make a loud thump on the hardwood. The last thing he saw was red and green.

Thump. Thump. Thump.

Jack opened his eyes, adjusting to the bright light. He stretched as if he had awoken in his own bed, but the smell of metal and blood engulfed him. Jack sprung up from the hard mattress, and let out an ear-splitting scream. Hovering over him was a group of identical women: pale-faced, beady-eyed and curly black hair. Their thin lips extended into wide smiles, exposing crooked fangs. They grabbed Jack and dragged him out of the humid room, speaking in quick and excited whispers. Jack squinted at the hallway. It was now radiating with bright, beautiful lights. He struggled in their hold as he approached large double doors. Standing in the front was the first girl he met, sneering at him with her red and green eyes.

"He's here." She opened the door and in the center of the room was a somber woman, crouched in a tall and bedazzled throne. Her head tilted down to her lap, but her penetrating eyes shook Jack to his core.

Vanity and greed feeds the queen, he thought.

The women tossed him at her feet and exited the room. Jack trembled as the elderly woman leaned her fragile head from side to side, observing him closely and carefully. The lights in the ballroom flickered violently— a showcase of red and green.

Jack stumbled back, and struggled to run to the door. He yanked the handle, but the door wouldn't budge.

Thump. Thump.

He could feel the woman's warmth behind him, but he refused to turn around. His sweaty palms gripped the door handle, and he gritted his teeth.

Piercing howls echoed around the room, but the woman's cackle managed to overwhelm the chaos. A flash of a silver lunged through Jack's chest, launching him to the wall.

Jack winced from the pain; his blood-curdling cry ending the war of horror. The chill flowed through his veins once again, but this time, he did not question the feeling. A streak of red and green blurred his vision until the woman crouched over him. Her blood-red lips widened as she showed him her canines. Jack's tongue rolled over his own instinctively.

Jack Vante, 1999.

HER

By Vivian Tang

My one and only love,
I will always wait for you.
Like the birds that fly south for the winter,
When will I see you again?

I long for your touch,
I want to feel your heartbeat against mine,
But I only grasp the air around me
when you are gone.
When will I see you again?

I miss you so much,
Your red dress vibrant
among the endless waves of the ocean,
Your grace and beauty
as you dance along the blue desert.
When will I see you again?

I have foolish hope
that you will return one day,
But where there is hope,
there is always hardship.
Where there is happiness,
there is always despair.
When will I see you again?

If our fate collides once more,
No matter where we are,
I want to see you again.

ARDENT
By Thanh Le

for the girls whose love is not understood

T.
They call our love a bouquet of roses,
because to them they see a garden of
bumblebees, sparrows, and water hoses.

True, our secret place, our sanctuary
is the garden with the apple tree swing,
but they know not of our intimacy.

Two women hold hands. Those who do not learn
our love, see an image of purity.
They don't know that she makes my heart burn.

The love we share is not one of sunshine
that's eternal. The fires in the heart burn
with passion, but also fury. That's fine.

N.
Next to you I stand, and I wish I could
show to everyone my bright love for you
but they'll misunderstand it as all good.

Nervously, I declare that love is more
than tender affections and red roses,
also tears, fears, and drowning at seashore.

Nearly everyone knows that but when they
see me and she, all of the sudden our
love is unlike their own to our dismay.

E.

Ephemeral—that word does not portray
our love, because my passion, affections
are Eternal. Even if our paths stray.

Every time you laugh and smile I adore
you even more as I could never have
enough, so I love you more than before.

Endless streams of complex feelings for you
that I ponder about when we sit on
our swing under the apple tree—just two.

Even if there was one slice left of my
favorite blueberry pie, I would wait
for you so we could share it—you and I.

D.

Dreaming of the day when I may let free
the breath I've been holding so that I may
freely love you unconditionally.

Do people know that we are not paintings
of superficial flower fields and trees?
Do they know we are not just pretty things?

R.

Resting on our swing, a sweet melody
of flutes and violins because alone
we, lovers, create our own symphony.

Running away with you is a dream so
very sweet, as I want nothing more than
to be free of those whispers so shallow.

A.

A love like ours, we know not how to cry
as we have been told to hold the burdens
of others, our hearts close, but don't know why.

A pair of girls plaster on shining smiles
since our vulnerability is shamed.
After they learn, their love will travel miles.

And so we learn to leave behind what we
have been taught about how we should behave
because then our love will flourish, we'll see.

A code, one unknown to other lovers,
will help me deliver my love to you.
Amid apple blossom petals, love endures.

ATLAS'S GUIDE TO HOLDING UP THE WORLD
By Hien Phan

ATLAS STANDS AT THE entrance of the underworld, takes a deep breath, and throws himself in.

Leaves fall gracefully with the autumn wind, waving hellos and weaving goodbyes in the breeze.

A group of people gather towards the center of an underground cave.

"What are we going to do about the monsters above?" they whisper, huddled together like a pile of raked leaves. "What *can* we do about it?"

"A little prayer to give us hope, perhaps." Someone takes out a baby's shoe. "For any life that may be preserved, that they may see an end to this destruction."

Another person snorts. "Pray to whom? Any God whatsoever has abandoned us on this wretched world." His voice cracks. "Whoever they are, they've left us to *die* without rain, without water, without so much as even a source of food while monsters ravage our villages and take our wives and kill our children and...and—"

"Settle down, Lulire." He wipes his tears with an already saturated tissue. "We are upset that our village has been destroyed as well. The most we can do now is hope that Atlas completes his mission and saves us all."

The people drape blankets over each other, occasionally flinching when the dirt ceiling rumbles and shakes with distant roars.

"Mama?" A child pokes her head out from underneath her cover. "What's Mr. Atlas doing?"

"He's doing something very important," says the mother. "He's on his way to making a wish with a spirit."

"Why is it so special?"

"Each person can only make one wish, and that wish is very hard to obtain. Most people don't return successfully, but Atlas has agreed to use his wish to send the monsters away."

The others continue to murmur amongst themselves, looking over the small civilization that has formed around them underground. The network sustains itself with a trickling stream and some roots for food, enough to get by, but all long to feel the autumn breeze that binds people together for warmth. Shared cups of hot chocolate will drift in and out of their dreams until they can hold hands and laugh with each other again.

Frost settles on their tongues during winter to keep thoughts encased in ice, never to be communicated.

Atlas had lied to them.

Really, they had it coming. Who doesn't have a personal wish? It's *their* fault for assuming he had nothing to live for.

When he finally emerges from below the surface, bioluminescent roses spring from the ground and tug at his ankles. He dusts himself off and stretches out any last aches before he finds the strength to continue down a zig-zag path. Memories play back in his mind— how they had picked him up from his corner of the cave and asked for his well-being, to which he had replied, "No, sir, I don't have any plans should the monsters suddenly disappear."

"You do not have any family to return to? No job, no dream?"

"No, sir."

"Then we have a favor to ask of you." They handed him one shoe, small enough to fit in his palm, and sent him off. "Bring this back when you save us."

A vague answer is easily misunderstood, so Atlas plots his opportunity to wish for his lover, ashen gray in a coffin, to come back.

Now he treks down the path where marigolds bloom and lights twinkle on the leaves. He notices how bright the lights are, making the space ahead resemble a winter field dappled with snow. As he continues, his thoughts meander to several different places, from weather to a recollection of his favorite memories with his lover.

He shivers. Weather. Atlas rubs his arms and exhales sharply, though it isn't enough to form puffs of steam. Perhaps he should have asked for another jacket or something to shield himself from the chill.

As he ventures further, he notices that the road starts to fade away, resembling less of Persephone's garden and more like Hades's domain. When Atlas reaches the places where the flowers become scarce, he picks a glowing marigold and tucks it into his pocket. Just a little something to put on his lover's grave when he returns.

If he returns.

Atlas shakes the thoughts from his mind and wonders how much longer this journey will last. Surely there must be some monster lying ahead? Or a terrifying creature waiting to eat him up? He trips over a rock and curses. Lifting his head up, Atlas notes that he is face to face with shiny mushrooms. Ah, so where the flowers wilt, the mushrooms thrive. They take care of the fallen, cleaning up the decomposing life into new earth, much like how the winter snow buries their life for a new season. He stands up again, admiring the little button-tops from above, and continues walking, hoping for a speedy journey because, god, his legs ache.

His heart aches too, from the shame that he brings with him. But he treks on anyways.

Flowers bloom and peek from the earth, unfamiliar with their surroundings as they push their way up.

With every step he takes, the path brightens until he reaches an illuminated room with a pool in the center. Before it, a sign sticks up from the rich soil, but he ignores it for the water. It sparkles as if reflecting the night sky. When he looks at his mirrored face, he spots someone next to him and whips his head around. A glassy figure shimmers before him, making him gasp.

"Atlas," sings a sweet voice, echoing throughout the cavern.

"Gais?"

"What are you doing here?"

Atlas explains his mission.

"You've always been a hero." Gentle laughter, twinkling like bells, lifts Atlas's heart.

"I can be your hero again, if you wish." He opens his arms for an embrace.

Again that laugh, yet Gais doesn't come closer. "You don't have to—I'm here now."

Atlas doesn't wait for the joy in his heart to settle as he gazes at his lover, oh so real and in front of him and *alive*, like a dream. He wants to, desperately wants to reach out and tousle his brown hair and whisper loving words and so much more, just as they used to do. "So I have to ask—what are you doing here? You've never been fond of water, after all."

"That doesn't matter." Gais leans in for a kiss then backs away playfully. "So as long as we are together, that is what truly matters."

Atlas nods and talks about a plethora of subjects—when they were young and played with sticks and stones and no one hurt each other up until their first kiss, how it had tasted like nectar from a flower and honey from a bee. His voice breaks when he recalls how far his heart fell when he desperately called Gais's name as he took his last breaths after a futile attempt to save their village.

His lover softly mentions how he wants to go back.

Atlas agrees.

He's alright with this fantasy, he thinks, as Gais laughs along with him. Atlas would like to stay like this forever, together in their own world.

Gais whispers a gentle suggestion that they should head towards the pool again. Atlas doesn't deny the request, and scoots closer to the edge. They both peer into the mirrored sky and admire how perfect they are next to each other, though Gais's messy hair can cause a mother to fret and Atlas's face is powdered with dust.

Atlas thinks about how his hands desperately want to tangle together with Gais's, and he tries to do so, but his hand goes right through.

Ah, it really is a dream, after all. Approaching a nightmare, perhaps, when he counts the warnings. The laughter that twinkles like bells now rings like death knells as Atlas stands up quickly.

"Are you afraid of me?" His lover's voice is still soothing to listen to, but Atlas's heart pounds.

"I don't"—Atlas backs away—"know you." The time that he had spent with Gais—or rather, his apparition—leads him to draw the conclusion that perhaps this isn't the Gais he once knew.

"Come." Gais tugs on his shirt playfully. "Let's go back to the water."

Atlas glances over at the sign. "A wish you shall make, a test you shall take; fallen are the ones who fail, and risen are the ones who prevail." Whatever test this is, it's making his heart ache with pins and fear and arrows and tears.

It hurts. It hurts so much. This unfamiliarity with someone he had planned to couple a ring with—oh, it hurts so much.

On the eve of summer's day, the waters shimmer, and though they reflect the summer's light, realization dawns with transparency.

"You're not my real lover," Atlas whispers, his voice cracking. "Gais is *dead*. He isn't coming back, no matter how much I wish for it."

"I'm here though. I'm here with you."

"Yet you are not." Tears run down his cheeks. "I understand what I must do. Please, cease this!" Atlas yells, and the caverns echo back his sorrows. "*Please.*"

Where Gais stood, there lies a blooming forget-me-not. Another spirit without form floats forward and beckons. "You have passed the trial. What is it that you wish for?" The spirit holds up two hands. "Your lover, or your world?"

Even now, Atlas reaches out for Gais, but he hesitates. *He is gone*, he repeats to himself. *Gone, cannot be returned to how he used to be, only a fabrication of mind.* His journey here, originally to exploit the opportunity given to him, falls flat, for the consequences of bringing back his lover may be too much for him to handle. He loves Gais, and Gais loves him, but it begs the question: will they be as happy as he envisions them to be? Dancing under the stars and listening to his laugh that twinkles like bells, sharing kisses and love words under the starry sky? He hesitates again.

And makes his decision.

"I bid you farewell. Journey back safely, risen one."

Leaves fall gracefully with the autumn wind, waving hellos and weaving goodbyes in the breeze.

It's been about a year since people have returned to the surface. A pair of baby shoes hangs at the entrance of their town. From the ground sprouts houses and buildings, stores and life again. Sometimes the roofs falter and a wall collapses, but then people laugh and joke about it, how it looks like raked leaves. Just like how it used to be.

Atlas takes part of the construction, admiring how the chilly breeze caresses his cheeks like a greeting. His scarf billows in the wind and covers his face, but he moves it to keep working. After all, nothing can stop him from asking for a cup of hot chocolate afterwards.

"Well done, hero." Lulire claps his back and whistles. "Boy, this is going to take a *long* time to rebuild."

Atlas looks around the growing village and nods.

After the day's work is over, the moon rises to bid everyone goodnight. Atlas smiles and walks a distance or so to a graveyard and spots the glowing marigold and forget-me-not. He brings a watering can and sprays a bit of water over a tomb that reads, "Gais. Died bravely protecting our town." He fondly thinks of the time that they used to be together.

But perhaps that is how the story of heroes is meant to end. One protects the earthly life, and the other journeys to hold up the world, and they love each other until the end. He's alright with that.

For now, Atlas bids his lover goodnight and returns to his newly-built house.

DUMB LOVE

By Kelly Ho

CHARACTERS

DANA, early 20's

ARON, mid 20's, Dana's best friend of ten years and the receiving end of Dana's one sided feelings

SASHA, mid 20's, Aron's girlfriend of three years

Note: **DANA'S CONSCIOUSNESS** *is an actual character. She is unnoticed by everyone except* DANA.

SETTINGS

HOSPITAL ROOM (INSIDE AND OUTSIDE)

HOSPITAL WAITING ROOM

I

LEFT HALF OF THE STAGE.

(*Lights switch on this half of the stage, showing a* HOSPITAL WAITING ROOM)
(DANA *rushes into the room, trying to follow* ARON *who is on a gurney, being wheeled into surgery*)

NURSE: Miss you are not allowed to enter.

DANA: But I need to know if he's alright! I—

NURSE: What is your relation with the patient?

DANA (*pausing before murmuring*): I am his best friend.

NURSE: I'm sorry miss, but only family may enter.
NURSE exits stage where a sign points, saying "emergency room this way"

DANA (*Whispering to herself, facing the audience*): I'm his best friend.

DANA'S SUBCONSCIOUS: That's a fact that will never change … stupid … you're his best friend … remember your limits.

DANA (*sighs, turns to the door*): That's right … I should stay in my place.

LIGHTS DIM. (*Spotlight on Dana who paces back and forth, downstage.*)

DANA: It's been two hours already. I hope he's okay.

ENTERS DOCTOR

DANA (*running up to the doctor*): Doctor how is he?

DOCTOR: He's stable, for now. He has kidney failure and needs a transplant as soon as we can find a donor.

DANA: Transplant? Me! I'll do it.

LIGHTS OFF.

II
RIGHT HALF OF THE STAGE.
(*The lights are turned on the right half of the stage and show the* INSIDE OF A HOSPITAL WARD DAY)

(*Dana approaches Aron, unconscious on the hospital bed*)
DANA (*takes a seat on the chair next to his bed and begins to pray with her eyes shut and hands tightly clasped together.*)

ARON (*Finally wakes up and lets out a cough.*)

DANA (*Leaps forward to hug Aron*): You're alive!

ARON (*Smiles and lets out a chuckle*): Be quiet, can you? You're going to let the entire hospital know.

DANA (*Looks embarrassed.*): Sasha's on her way. I called her earlier.

ARON (*Smiles and pulls Dana in for a hug.*): Indeed. You're my best friend.

DANA (*Wriggling around trying to escape Aron's embrace*)**:** Let me—

ARON: Shh…just five minutes okay?

(DANA *stops her struggling; her face is to the audience*)

DANA'S CONSCIOUS (O.S.): You know he just thinks of you as his friend right?

DANA: Yeah…I know.

DANA'S CONSCIOUS (O.S.): Then why are you getting nervous?

DANA: That's because—well—shut up!

DANA'S CONSCIOUS (O.S.): Stop it Dana. Face reality, would you?

DANA: I know…but I love him…

DANA'S CONSCIOUS (O.S.): And that's why you're dumb. You know very clearly he doesn't feel the same way.

DANA: But I'm happy to just be by his side—

DANA'S CONSCIOUS (O.S.): Until when Dana? Until when are you going to be happy?

(*Dana became quiet as she hears those words.*)

DANA: No…I cannot truly be happy for him when I am thrown aside. I am selfish like that…because I'm human. I don't care about what the rest of the world says, humans all are selfish.

BACK IN THE HOSPITAL WARD
(*Dana looks up at Aron's face.*)

DANA (*turns to the audience*)**:** Can I just give you up? Can I give up these feelings I've had since way back when?

ARON: Hey, I know I'm handsome, but you're disturbing my 5 minutes. (ARON *smiles lightly with his eyes still shut.*)

DANA (*laughingly*): Whatever, idiot.

ARON: No need to be shy…buttface. (*Aron laughs. Dana buries her face in Aron's shirt.*)

DANA (*monologue to herself*): Just a while more…I'll just love you on my own…just for a while more…

DANA: Tell me why I'm your best friend again?

ARON: 'Cause you love me.
(*Dana's eyes tear up, wetting Aron's shirt. Aron chuckles.*)

DANA: Stop laughing.

ARON (*laughing while petting Dana's head*): It must be that time of the month.

(DANA *chuckles and punches Aron's shoulder.*)

ARON: My little baby girl is already grown up but still cries so easily. (*Aron ruffles Dana's hair*)

DANA: Shut up, stupid. (*Dana smacks Aron's hand away*)

ARON: Oooh! But she's always so mean. (*Aron releases Dana from the hug and sits up. He smiles and turns to give Dana a kiss on the head.*)

ARON: I love you, bud.
(*Aron turns to the door that just opened, revealing* SASHA.)

DANA (*Whispers to herself*): Me too, you dummy.

SASHA (*Runs to hug Aron*): Are you okay? Are you hurt? Do you know how scared I was when I heard you passed out at work?

DANA (*Pokes Aron's leg and points towards the door, mouthing the words 'good-bye'*)

ARON (*Smiles and nods, before turning his attention back to his girlfriend Sasha*): It was kidney failure. The good news is that they've already found a donor.

OUTSIDE — ARON'S HOSPITAL WARD (*Divided from the inside using a wall*)

(DANA *leans on the door after closing it and falls to the ground in tears.*)
DANA (*whispering*): What am I to you?

DANA'S CONSCIOUS (O.S.): This is exactly what I warned you about.

DANA: Shut up…I'm not in the mood.

DANA'S CONSCIOUS (O.S.): I told you not to fall in this dumb trap. It's only going to hurt you.

DANA: But I can't help it.

DANA'S CONSCIOUS (O.S.): Just give it up. This dumb love.

(*A* NURSE *comes from down the hall.*)
NURSE: Are you Dana Gladwells?

DANA (*Nods*): Yes, I am.

NURSE: The doctor needs to inform you of the papers you need to give for the kidney donation.

DANA: Ahh…yes.

NURSE: The doctor is waiting for you in his office down the hall to the right.

DANA: Alright, I'll be right there.

NURSE (*nods and exits*)

DANA (*through Aron's ward's window, whispering to herself*): Love… what a stupid thing. (*Dana shakes her head as tears stream down her face.*)

WONDER
by Alyssa Starnes

Trapped in my own home
For more than four years
Watching other kids play outside
Brought me to tears
I took a look out my window
To see the blue sky
But the glare of the glass
Made the happiness within me die
The doctors came into my room
And they bring my mother too
They tell me something amazing
It was the best news
I could finally walk outside
For the first time ever
I rolled outside in a wheelchair
And stared at the sky forever

THE PERSISTENCE OF MEMORY
By Kelvin Pham
inspired by "The Persistence of Memory" by Salvador Dali

Four forsaken clocks melt in a vast, desolate land
Where the sands of memory erode all traces
of the existence of all worrisome things
Brought about by pedantic men
in their mundane, occupied lives.

It is a haunting, hapless dream state
That no man could have imagined.
Against the pedestal, a lone tree leans,
Bearing an ill clock, hanging over his companions
who lie restless on the charred, umber ground.

Faraway in the desert,
a raised, slate platform wait by a sea of nothing.
A sheer bluff stand tirelessly by the shore,
Hoping that someday the tides will gnaw her away,
Until the very last speck of her reality fade into oblivion.

What of those timepieces
Abandoned in their deteriorated form—
Their ultimate presence incomprehensible—
Kept under the palms of sand,
Lingering until they are set free from their prison of sepia heat?

What of anything
Has any certain meaning to our drudgery
If we cannot truly escape it?
What of everything
Is worth anything?

SEA OF A THOUSAND WORDS
By Aithy Nguyen

CHRISTIAN STUMBLED ACROSS THE ship deck surrounded by shouts and wails. He struggled to make his way to the railing while frantic passengers shoved and elbowed him. Only half of the small red lifeboats remained. Mass panic ensued as everyone tried to board them.

Christian's pace slowed, his breath quickening by the second. He turned to the right and left and circled back around. There weren't any boats left for him to board. All were being filled to the maximum. Yet the number of people still on the sinking ship did not seem to lessen.

He pushed through the crowds of people who looked overwhelmed at the events around them, all hope for himself diminished. He stumbled to a clear section of the deck, and leaned against the railing, inhaling deeply. He looked around. Some people ran past him, but he was soon all by himself. He wept for his inevitable death.

The boats disappeared by the minute, dropping into the dark sea. Twenty lifeboats remaining turned to sixteen, sixteen turned to seven, seven turned to one. He stared at it sorrowfully, thinking about his brother, Benjamin. What did his brother look like nowadays? Did he finally find a wife and start a family?

"May I join you for a moment?"

He jumped and turned to see a woman in a thick fur coat now standing beside him. She looked no more than thirty, her face lined with light wrinkles. He nodded. She stepped closer, wrapping her coat tighter around her body. They stared at the screaming mob near the remaining lifeboat.

"Ma'am?" He tilted his head. He didn't know what she wanted, nor why she was as calm as she was in the situation. The floor shook, followed by the sound of wood cracking and men and women screaming.

He and the extravagantly dressed woman lost their balance and fell onto the deck. There wasn't much time left. The last lifeboat descended and the ship was quickly becoming engulfed by the moonlit sea. They both held tightly onto the foot of a wooden bench bolted to the deck as everything slowly tilted to the right. The ship made a loud, drawn out groan as if the hull was being torn apart. Water splashed onto the deck. He heard a sniffle beside him and turned to meet the gaze of the woman.

"My husband left me," she said. She was tearing up, but maintained her gaze into the distance. "We got separated when the boat began to sink. He abandoned me like I was nothing to him."

Christian felt a pang in his heart, even though his dire situation was no better. He did not know her husband, nor anything about her life. Yet, he couldn't help but feel sorry. Her voice weakened as she began to shed tears.

"He…" she started. Her sobs got in the way of her speech. "He took my child."

He watched her in agony, unsure of what to say. As the ship continued to tip to the right, his tightened his grip on the bench leg.

"My boy," she cried. "He took my boy and left me behind."

He could barely hear her as her voice trailed off. Loud groans of bending metal and shredding wood echoed beneath them. The ship jolted back to the left scon after the last lifeboat had lowered into the sea. The remaining passengers on deck scattered, screaming to find additional life rafts on the deck below.

Christian stood up, steadied his balance, and held out his hand, offering to help her to her feet. Turbulent waves rocked the ship and splashed aboard. She reached for his hand.

The ocean drenched them with each splash. She leaned against his body while she coughed and wiped the seawater from her face. He gently patted her back and tried to distract her from the rising water level.

"I know your husband," he lied.

Her gaze shifted to him. "You know my Richard?" She frowned, but her eyes gleamed with hope.

He nodded. "He said he loves you very much, and will return to you with your son very soon." He wasn't sure if she would believe him, but in her delusional state, she did. The woman smiled, more tears escaping her swollen eyes.

"Richard," she whispered, "I knew he would come back." She wiped her face. "He's bringing my boy to me. I have to wait for him." She brushed off Christian's arm and gripped the railing, looking around in anticipation.

Christian would have protested, if it wasn't for the look of solace he saw on her face. He stood beside her and closed his eyes. He had accepted his fate.

It was faint, so very faint. At first he thought it was an illusion, or maybe a trick of the moonlight. But when he opened his eyes, he could not believe what he saw in the distance. There, a flicker of dark red, with one passenger waving hands in his direction, was a lifeboat, a lifeboat that could be his salvation. He ran towards it, pulling the woman with him. They would have to jump into the ocean and swim to reach it. The others aboard the ship were too consumed in their panic to notice another lifeboat. He felt relieved to know that God had not forsaken him after all. He got ready to jump, but before he did, he felt a firm tug on his arm.

"I can't leave," she said. "Richard is coming for me."

He realized that she was still wrapped up in the lie he had told earlier. Christian felt a pang of guilt build in his chest, "No, ma'am, he isn't coming. Not here, not now. We need to get you to safety. Please, come, there isn't much time." He moved to jump, and was again held in place.

Her eyes were dilated, her breaths ragged. "I told you." Her voice turned stern. "I am waiting for Richard."

Every minute arguing with her was a wasted minute of delay. The boat was becoming harder to see as it drifted farther away. He could barely see the outline of the person aboard.

No, this would not be where it ended. Whatever it took, he would make sure he would see his brother Benjamin, again. He would not fail, again, like he had done years ago.

Christian pulled free of the woman's grasp. "Yes," he said. "Wait here. Richard will come." With that, he quickly climbed over the railing, jumped into the dark sea, and swam his way to the little red lifeboat in the distance.

It was difficult to endure. The freezing waters were almost unbearable as was the burning sensation of salt in his eyes and mouth. He saw the lifeboat clearly though, getting closer and more vibrant in color. Fifty treads, or maybe sixty. He had lost track, but it didn't matter. He was determined to get to it, even if he died trying.

Nancy tried to help him by urging the boat closer, but she was not strong enough, and only delayed it from drifting away slightly if not at all. He was a strong fellow though. She watched him break against the waves shattering them like glass. Each advance split the water into glittering jewels. It was a battle forged in pure perseverance, and he was victorious. He collided with the wooden walls of the lifeboat. Nancy leaned out to help him aboard. He held on to her desperately as he clambered onto the lifeboat. He fell onto his back with a loud thump, breathing raggedly. She could hear him struggle to relay words.

"We…" he said. He took rapid breaths. "We have to go back. We have to go back." He coughed up water. "There's a woman…" He tried to rise, sank back down coughing.

She put her palm on his chest. "You need to rest, sir. You are out of breath and can't overexert yourself."

It was too late for that. He went silent and still.

"Sir?" she asked. "Sir, can you hear me?" She slapped his cheek but he did not stir. "Dear lord." She let out a breath of relief as the sound of a beating heart echoed in her ear.

Christian's body ached all around. He opened his eyes and found a sting greeting him awake. He blinked consecutively and held his hand over his eyes to shade them from the burning sun.

"You are awake, finally," he heard a voice say. He turned to see a girl beside him. She was no older than twenty perhaps, but definitely not older than he. Her dark hair was tangled and tied back messily. She wore a long sleeved cream dress, torn at the hem. He concluded that she was not from a wealthy family, as her dress looked as if it was made from some cheap fabric. She placed her hand on his forehead. "You were out for two days," she said as she put her hand back down on her lap. "Feverish for a time but it subsided quickly. Do you remember anything that happened?"

He bit his lower lip and gazed downward. "I wanted to go back for someone," he simply said. He was waiting for her to ridicule him, but instead she smiled in understanding.

"I saw men turn into barbarians," she said. "I saw women trade in their dignity for savagery. By the end of the day people are out for their own necks. You have shown great courage to have done otherwise."

She had not said much, but it gave him the warmth of a thousand welcoming words. He met her gaze again, and she sorrowfully smiled.

"Was she a lover?"

He let out a cough and a choke. "No, no, nothing like that." He hesitated. "To be honest, I don't know why I wanted to save her. I didn't know her in the slightest."

"But there was nothing you could have done even if you were still awake."

"I could have saved her. We could have gone back."

She shook her head. "This is the captain's private lifeboat. There is only room for two passengers."

He surveyed the boat. He had not noticed before, but it was true. It was smaller than a regular passenger lifeboat. Made for only two. "There were many more who were drowning," he said. "Why save me?"

She shrugged. "You were the closest person, and if I had signaled to the others, the boat would have been swarmed. You were close to being alone so it worked in my favor."

He sighed. "I still wanted to save that woman. I told her I would come back but ended up leaving. What I despise most in this world is the feeling of abandonment, because I've lived with it for so many years, and I went and did it to her. God, she probably died thinking I was a complete liar." He closed his eyes for a while, hoping to clear his clouded mind.

"Would you have gone back and sacrificed your place for a woman who means nothing to you?" she asked.

The question was left unanswered, but they both knew his answer.

They were in the middle of the ocean. There was nothing to be seen but the blue waters surrounding them. They were running low on provisions. Four barrels of water and an unused first aid kit. No food. *We would only make it for another week,* Nancy thought, and she was being generous. It had been four days out to sea. She would spend her time rationing out their water supply. She would try, on some occasion, to make conversation with him, but he wasn't the type to say anything that didn't seem necessary to say. On the fifth sunrise Nancy had decided she had had enough of his silence.

"What's your story?" she asked.

He stopped picking at his fingernails. "I haven't the slightest idea what you mean, ma'am."

She had asked for his name once, but he only sighed and turned away from her. She would not oblige him this time. "Nancy," she stated. "I think we have spent enough time together to pass the formalities."

He stared blankly. "Christian."

She relaxed her shoulders. He was in a better mood today. "Well then, Christian, tell me, what is your story?"

"Clearly, you did not understand the first time, Nancy. I don't know what you mean."

She sighed. "Let's start from the beginning then. Why did you board the Pentigod Ark?"

He was silent at first, but seeing that there was no other alternative, he relented. "You first."

She beamed at the thought of a real conversation. "My birthday was the tenth of February. Every year my parents would grant me one wish. Each of those years, I would ask for passage to another place on my father's map. He was a sailor, you see, and he had been all across the globe. It was only natural for me to want to see the world as he did. This year, I asked to see America. I've heard so much about it. It is a place where dreams come true, and where people get second chances.

England was beginning to become rubbish to me so I needed a way out." She took a sip of their precious water before continuing.

"My father agreed to take my mother and me."

There was a pause. He noticed her eyes began to water. "What happened to them?"

She cleared her throat and wiped her wet face. "My mother had an accident nine years ago. She hadn't been able to walk since."

"That's why you left her behind." It wasn't a question.

"My father could not leave her. She had wanted to save us both but he would not allow it. He had loved her too much to live without her, even with me still alive."

"You've got a captain's lifeboat," he stated. He waited for her to stop crying. "You're not any ordinary sailor's daughter, are you?"

She gulped, her throat burning from being parched.

"You're the captain's daughter."

"I am the youngest of two boys. Benjamin is the eldest. By twenty-two, he had become a successful physician and made good coin from his achievements." Christian shifted in his seat while she drank some more water. "I looked up to Benjamin. He was always the better brother, of course, the brother I wish I was, and I strived to be him." Christian paused.

"Go on," Nancy said.

"The year after he went abroad to further study medicine, he decided to come back to visit home. I was anticipating his arrival for weeks and finally I was able to see him once more. He came through the door in a dark coat. I remember how thick it was, how it smelled, how it loosely coiled around his body.

"After him came his new fiancé. Her name was Fiona. She was tall, slender, and her hair was tied up but arranged so that some of the golden strands framed her freckled oval face. I noticed because Benjamin had a preference for women with them." He didn't know exactly why he was telling her this story. He had never told anyone, let alone someone he had just met. Regardless, he continued. "At dinner, he shared with the family his findings and experiences with his profession. I did not have much taste in the field, so I didn't remember much of what he said. Instead, I spoke to Fiona. She was the friendly sort, similar to you, Nancy."

She snorted. "And definitely not similar to you."

He ignored her comment. "It started off with small talk. I asked how old she was, where she was from, how she met Benjamin. I learned later that Benjamin would be staying for two months to plan for the wedding since they had planned to wed in Manchester rather than her hometown in America. He was mostly busy with the work because he was doing it alone.

"Fiona told him she wanted to spend time getting to know his family more instead. That did not happen. Every day for those two months Benjamin would run morning errands while Fiona would disappear, coming back just before he did. I tried taking her to a local bakery to buy her my favorite buttered pastry, but she had always refused.

"I had no intention whatsoever, other than to please my brother. He would be proud that I had at least tried to make his woman happy. I did fancy her though, really I did. I had already considered her a sister, and a part of my family." He looked distant as he spoke.

"So what happened?" Nancy asked.

"One day I decided to follow her. She was extremely fast, but I managed to tail her without being seen. I found myself tracking her to a nearby inn. I did find it tremendously odd that she would be there. She was staying with us after all. Once I was inside, I followed her to room seventy-four. I've hated those numbers ever since. She went in, but I hovered outside, listening to the ever so soft voices from the inside.

"It was then I discovered Fiona was not who I thought she was. The person occupying the room was a man named Alfred Tenner, a poor married man, and, her lover. They met at the inn to avoid suspicion. She never had feelings for Benjamin. She was only using him for her personal gain. After he would take her over to America, she would marry him as planned, and as soon as she did, she would take all his money and run off with Alfred to some place where they couldn't be found."

Nancy's mouth was wide open. "Oh my God."

He shut his eyes.

"That wicked witch."

He clenched his jaw.

"How old was she?"

"Twenty, same as me," he replied.

"And did your brother find out?"

He reopened his eyes. "I wouldn't hide something like this from him, even if I knew knowing would hurt him. As I quickly made my way to leave, I bumped into a maid delivering a tray of muffins. Fiona came out instantly at the sound of the fallen tray, and went red with rage when she saw me. That's when I ran for my life. She chased me all the way to my house. Fortunately, I was just a tad faster. I went in, closed the door, and locked her outside. She banged over and over, harshly. I remember my heart beating so fast I almost fainted. Moments later Benjamin came running. He was puzzled and went to let her in. I blocked his path, and as best I could, told him everything."

"And did he believe you?" she asked.

He shook his head. "Not even a word. He pushed me aside after calling me mad and opened the door. I had expected her to deny something. Anything. That would have given me some leverage. But she had only laughed. Benjamin asked her what we were doing, and she gave him the most ridiculous answer possible. Tag. We were playing tag. What was even more absurd was the fact that he believed her. So blinded by love, he believed that grown adults were out and about playing tag." He scoffed. "The next morning, she was gone. All her belongings, vanished, as if Benjamin had never brought a guest. The only thing left behind, was a goodbye letter, saying I had tried seduced her and that she could not sleep in a house where she was not safe, nor marry a man who had me as a brother. Benjamin, of course, did not take it lightly."

"How long ago?" she asked.

"Seven years," he replied. "After that day he never spoke to me again. He returned to America and never came back. My parents never forgave me, either. It was my fault they would never see their precious son again." He sat straighter. "That is why for the last seven years, I have worked. I have become the man he had wanted me to be. I studied, worked, and saved up enough coin to pay for this trip. I was going to America to find him and explain. It did not matter that he did not want to see me. I was going to make it right again. I was going to mend what I had broken." He had nothing else to say. He only felt his chest tighten in guilt.

"What you had broken?" she said. "You're an idiot, Christian."

He turned to her. "I beg your pardon?"

"Did you love her? Did you throw yourself to her? Did you beg her to leave your brother and marry you instead? No. No, you did not. He is the one at fault for thinking it is because of you that she left him. She lied and he believed her. That isn't your fault. What you said is not a crime, but the truth. He should have listened to you. Your parents may have not seen it, but I do, and I see nothing more than an innocent man who tried to protect his brother from an unfaithful woman."

Christian's lips were slightly parted.

"That woman. The one you wanted to save," she started, "You feel responsible, don't you? Just like you think it was your fault that your brother left, again you think it's your fault someone died."

He coughed. He had wanted to ask how much water was left, but couldn't find the strength to in his weakened state.

"Christian, you can't beat yourself up for everything unfortunate that happens in your life."

He was in disarray. He could not fathom what she had just said, or rather the fact that she could be right. He did not get to finish his thought when she called out.

"Land!" she shot up from where she sat, making the boat rock from side to side. She pointed to his right and as he turned, he could not be more joyous.

She raced to help him descend onto the sand. The sun still blazed in the clear blue sky. People from the ports rushed to them as well.

"Help, please," she called out. "We are from the Pentigod Ark. The ship has sunken. We have been at sea for several days."

They both could barely stand upright. The men led them to a nearby cabin and offered them heavy blankets to cover themselves. It was warm inside. She had never been so grateful for a simple fireplace. They sat down and set out in front of them on the wooden table was a cup of a warm liquid.

"It's herbal tea," an elderly woman said. "Have a sip. It relieves the body."

That it did, and Nancy shortly found herself falling in a deep sleep.

Christian was tired, eyes struggling to stay open, but he did not sleep as Nancy did. After a while, she rose from her slumber. She stretched her arms in her blanket.

"That felt nice." She yawned. "First peaceful rest I've had in days."

He had thought about her while she was out, worry on his mind.

"Where will you go when they take us back home?" he asked.

She didn't answer right away. "Well, I…" She hesitated. "I have an uncle. He…"

He arched a brow. "He what?"

She looked him in the eye. "I can't live with him. Every night he wastes his time carousing, bringing a different woman home every night. I would rather die than live with that man. Other than him though, I have no one else."

He nodded. "I see. It'll all be sorted. I'm sure you won't have to deal with him." All was quiet for a good couple minutes. "It's not your doing, you know."

She tilted her head. "Whatever do you mean?"

"I know you feel you weren't enough to save them. Your parents."

She faltered. "Father stayed back because of Mother. He didn't even look me in the eyes when he let me go."

"He let you go. He chose you over himself. If he were really as selfish as you say he is, he would have boarded the boat with your mother and left you to die instead."

She did not look convinced.

"You told me not to beat myself up for every unlucky thing that happens to me. Now I say it to you. Don't make something that wasn't your fault cause you grief. A captain always goes down with his ship does he not?"

She sucked in a breath. "At least they had each other."

He reached for her hand and gave it a gentle nudge. "I've thought about what you said and I want to thank you for being the first person genuinely on my side." He looked Nancy in the eyes. "I'm still going to America. I've come this far and I want to do what I set out to do. I will find my brother and make amends with him."

She smiled. "Then do it. We have only been in each other's company for a few days; nevertheless, I have found you to be quite charming. Your brother can't stay mad at you forever. He simply just can't bring himself to."

His cheeks reddened, but he felt more settled than embarrassed. "Come with me."

Her eyes widened. "To America?"

"You were going there for a sense of adventure. It would have been your birthday gift. Why stop midway? And this ensures you won't have to live with your uncle. See America just once. See the place that has changed countless of lives as you say."

She was out of words, but soon found herself smiling, yet again. "It would be a waste of a trip to turn back now, wouldn't it?"

"Indeed it would."

PROCRASTINATION

By Thanhchau Chu

Procrastination
Is a magnet
Far stronger than
North and South poles.
It pulls us down
And forces us to make
Regretful decisions
That pain our heart and soul.
No matter how much
We try to resist
It is like defying gravity
It is out of our control.

Don't procrastinate,
It's not worth it!
Don't procrastinate,
Why does one do it?
Don't procrastinate,
Only the pain remains.
Don't procrastinate,
All your efforts would be in vain.
Don't procrastinate,
It is a big mistake
Don't procrastinate,
It'll only keep you awake.

Procrastination
It's an interesting idea
A fascinating thought
An intriguing thing
That everyone has fought.
The battle is real
It's difficult to win
But if you never give it a chance,
You've only got everything to lose;
It may be a hard choice,
But it's so easy to choose.

CHANCE

By Jennifer Ho

A golden cozy afternoon
Rays of sunlight beaming
on vivid surrounding green.

Refreshing rush of wind sweeps across
vast welkin blue sky
Blood red poppies glare
at the pearly white roses
through the opening
of a ragged hickory brown fence.

Hiding in shallow cracks
of that same fence
An amaranth pink daisy
waves gracefully
at its neighbors
and the radiant sun
for its beautiful chance.

DISTANCE
By HongAnh Nguyen

How does one grow apart
From the one they knew so well?
We were inseparable,
Day in and day out.

Wherever I was
There you were, too.
Anywhere we went,
Had to have room for two.

From the depth of the night,
To the early morning,
We were together,
Always calling and talking.

Why is it recently,
We've been drifting,
I don't see you,
Morning or evening.

Our conversations are drying,
Short, simple, unsatisfying.
I'm desperately trying to save,
But my effort seems to be lacking.

This is not what I wanted,
This is not what I imagined,
Can we go back,
To the way we used to be?

I sense a goodbye around the corner,
It's these I'm especially bad at,
Perhaps we can hold it off a bit longer,
So I can reminisce what we had.

There's not much time left,
Whittling down by the hour,
But if you stay here with me,
We'll make it last forever.

As I wish it is possible,
I know deep down it is not.
But keep me in your heart,
And it'll have been worthwhile.

OPPOSITE OF THE SUN
By Thanh Le

EPHERA OPENED HER BROWN eyes to see an unfamiliar blue sky adorned with whirlpools of white clouds. The young girl, entranced by the sight, lay there for several minutes staring at the sky. With arms by her side, she hummed "Ode to Joy." Upon hitting the final C note, Ephera turned her head to the side to find herself atop a bed of lilies.

"Oh, how pretty." Ephera sat up and gazed upon the white petals with light yellow centers. Never in her life did she have the chance to truly admire their beauty. She plucked one from the ground and placed it in her light brown hair. Ephera noticed white bandages wrapped around her head and gently removed them, allowing them to fly away in the wind. She stood up and giggled as she twirled around in the lily bed, her white cotton dress mimicking the blooming flowers. "I don't know where I am, but I'm glad I'm here."

A chatter came from the distance, causing Ephera to stop. A ferret ran towards her, jumped, and wrapped itself around her neck, nuzzling her cheek. Ephera laughed as its fur tickled her.

"You seem really familiar," she said, holding the ferret in her arms. "Do I know you?"

The ferret blinked in response.

"Alright then," she said. "How about I give you a name? Something cute, like Chiki."

The ferret squeaked and ran up Ephera's arms in order to lick her cheeks. The two ran around the flower fields, playing tag, making flower crowns, and cuddling without a care. Before Ephera knew it, the sun began to set. And now, she and Chiki were no longer near the bed of lillies.

"Uh-oh spaghetti-o's," she said. "It's getting late. I was having so much fun for once, but I need to get home." Ephera searched for a familiar path, but all she could see were flowers, trees, and a large mountain range in the sunset's orange gaze. "What should I do, Mama is going to be—"

Chiki jumped off Ephera's shoulder. On the ground, it pointed northeast with its nose, urging her to walk in that direction. Without hesitation the girl followed the ferret, walking through the flora. Even though it was nightfall, their road was clear and illuminated by the full moon. Whites, golds, light blues, and greenery glowed. Fireflies danced about the sky—tiny orbs of gold as beautiful as the stars.

"Wow. The sky's so clear. What's beyond it?" she asked Chiki, not expecting an answer.

The two walked for several more minutes in silence before reaching a small cottage. It was a quaint and simple structure. In the front yard stood a small garden adorned with flowers, fruits, and vegetables.

Ephera knocked on the mahogany door.

An elderly man with a full beard smiled as he opened the door. He placed his hands in the pockets of his blue coat. "Why hello. Are you lost, young girl? You seem to be a new person in this land."

"Hello Mister." Ephera gave a practiced bow to the old man. "Yes, I'm lost. Do you know how I can find my way back home?"

The old man flinched. "Well…erm…tell me, what's the last thing you remember before you came here?"

Ephera paused to think about the old man's question. Her memories were fuzzy of the previous day. "I think I was going for a walk to get groceries."

"I see," The old man replied. "You don't know, do you?"

"Huh? Know what, Mister?"

"Ah, don't worry about it for now. Unfortunately, I don't know the way to your home, but I can let you stay the night here, if you would like." The elderly man opened the door a little wider.

"I think I have to get home soon, or else my Mama will get super angry." Ephera twiddled her fingers together.

"It's much too dark out now to try to venture home. It's dangerous to be outside alone here at night, especially with a troubled heart."

Ephera stared at the ferret perched on her shoulders, and then back to the elderly man, frowning in thought. *It'll be okay, right? Mama won't get too mad, I hope.* Chiki jumped off her shoulders and bounded into the cottage without hesitation.

Ephera watched Chiki sit next to him. She looked up at the elderly man. "Okay Mister, and thank you for offering."

"You're such a polite young girl, aren't you? Oho! Anyways, you can call me Mr. Hector. What's your name?"

"My name is Ephera. It's nice to meet you, Mr. Hector."

"What a lovely name. Come inside now, I'll make you some hot chocolate."

Golden lights illuminated his house. The fireplace glowed, and before it was a lush green rug, two small desks, and two comfortable red chairs.

"Welcome to my humble abode. Make yourself at home, Ephera." Mr. Hector gestured to the two red chairs as he walked towards the kitchen. "I'll have you know, I have the softest chairs around, oho."

Ephera plopped herself on one of the red chairs, sinking into it. She smiled as she closed her eyes, imagining that she was lying on one of the fluffy clouds in the sky. Chiki lay on the arm of the same chair, and closed its eyes. When she opened her eyes, Ephera looked at the many paintings of scenery that dotted the house. She saw a hill that overlooked a seaside town, an ocean with bright coral reefs, an open plain with green grass moving in the wind, and a field of irises before a mountain.

Mr. Hector returned with two mugs of hot chocolate, handing one to Ephera.

"You have a very nice home, Mr. Hector." Ephera took a sip of hot chocolate. "This whole land is lovely."

"Indeed it is." Mr. Hector smiled. "I hope I can show him how lovely this place is soon."

"Who?"

"Ah, my husband. He's not here yet."

"Why's that? If he's your husband—" Ephera burned her tongue and was forced to stick it out to ease the pain. "He should be with you."

Mr. Hector laughed at the girl's ardent demeanor and ruffled the her hair.

"It's fine. He's just having a journey—experiencing life to his fullest before he comes home."

"Oh, alright. But if he doesn't come home, you should tell me. Then I'll fight him." Ephera formed a pair of fists, hitting the air with punches.

Mr. Hector let out another laugh, deeper and louder than the last. "You remind me of my daughter when she was your age. Both of you have a certain spirit—you can make anyone feel better."

"Really? I don't know about that. I never make my Mama happy."

Mr. Hector's gaze fell to the lily tucked in Ephera's short, brown hair. Her bright, brown eyes radiated hopes and dreams. Tears tugged at him.

"Mr. Hector, what's wrong? Why are your crying?" Ephera tugged on Mr. Hector's shirt. "Did I make you cry? I'm sorry."

Chiki awoke from its slumber, noticing the pain in both of their hearts. It hopped off the chair and began to wander around the room, leaving Ephera and Mr. Hector together.

"Oh, sweet child, please do not blame yourself for anything…" Mr. Hector dried his tears. "I'm simply an old man with a tender heart, is all. Come now, drink some of your hot chocolate."

"Are you sure about that? I don't know..." Ephera's gaze fell to the mug of hot chocolate. "It's just that—"

"Repeating blame gets you nowhere, Ephera. It only leads to obsessions and fixations. You're very young and a very nice girl, so do not blame yourself for something in your past." Mr. Hector's demeanor had changed. He placed his mug of hot chocolate down on the desk next to his chair. "Think about my words, Ephera. Sometimes, things happen that you can't control. "

My. Hector picked up his mug of coffee and took a sip. The two sat in tranquility. To have company after many years, filled Mr. Hector with such warmth—warmth that he hadn't felt in an eternity. He couldn't find it in himself to tell Ephera the truth, so for now he would enjoy their time together. Chiki returned to Ephera—its nose had a bit of ash on it.

"Mr. Hector." Ephera tightened her grasp on the mug. "How do I get home?"

"Are you sure you want to go home?" Mr. Hector looked at Ephera.

"Yes. Yes I do. In the end, it's still my home."

"I see." Mr. Hector stood up and pointed to one of the paintings. "If you travel to the eastern mountain, your answers will be there. Right now, we're on the western side of the land. There are two things you can do, little Ephera. Stay here with me and live a slow and peaceful life, or make the journey to the east. You'll meet lots of people, and some of them won't be nice at first, but through that journey, you will discover what you wish to know."

"If it's too dangerous, can I come back if I want to?"

"Of course. You're always welcome here."

The next morning, Mr. Hector gave Ephera a backpack full of food, water, and other essentials.

"Thank you." She hugged him. "I will never forget your kindness."

"Be safe on your journey now." Mr. Hector hugged her back as tears began to form. He ruffled her hair one more time. "Take this piece of paper—just in case you forget anything I told you."

She took the paper and bowed. "Make sure your husband comes back soon, okay?" Ephera said. If she walked at a reasonable pace on her journey to the east, Mr. Hector had said that she would reach town in a day's journey. In town, she was supposed to take the train "across the ocean."

"What do I mean when I say across the ocean? Well you'll just have to find out. I don't want to ruin the surprise." Mr. Hector gave a hearty chuckle.

"Do you know what he meant, Chiki?" Ephera asked. Chiki swayed its tail. "You do know, huh. You just don't want to tell me, either."

71

Ephera noticed a hastily written note, below the instructions she was given. The note insisted that she had to make it to town before the sun set, but he also wrote to "trust in Chiki if you can't make it to town in time."

At sunset, on the base of the hill, Ephera saw a sign that said "Spirit Town."

"Chiki, there it is." Ephera ran up the hill. From the top, she could see yellow and orange lights dotting the entire town, and people walking, talking, and shopping. In the distance, she saw the ocean. The sun was beginning to dip below the horizon, leaving strokes of orange in the water. Best of all, she saw the train: gliding across the water at full speed, leaving tiny waves behind. Chiki stared at the train until it, too, disappeared behind the horizon.

"That is amazing, Chiki. I can't wait to ride on it." Ephera jumped up and down several times. "Oh, but it would be so nice to explore the town a little bit first, yes?"

While she was engrossed by the sight, Ephera heard heavy footsteps behind her. She turned and was face to face with a, black bear-like creature with glowing, red eyes. Oil dripped from its fur, disintegrating when it hit the ground. Ephera clutched Chiki as she slowly backed away.

"Maybe it'll leave us alone if we're quiet," she whispered. Chiki began to hiss at the creature, trying to get free of Ephera's grasp. "Chiki, don't do anything." Ephera tried to keep Chiki away from the bear-like creature, who was growling at the two. It stood up on its hind legs and roared. Ephera dropped Chiki to cover her ears. Now on the ground, Chiki ran to the creature and blasted it with a beam of light that flew from Chiki's mouth. The light vaporized the creature, leaving nothing but shadowy dust.

"Chiki." Ephera was stunned. "Chiki, what was that? You never told me that you were a magic ferret."

Chiki stood with its head and tail held high. Relieved to be safe from the monstrous bear, Ephera gave Chiki a hug.

The ferret twirled in circles and did a jig. Ephera giggled at the ferret's display.

A hiss from the darkness caused Ephera to turn around.

There, a giant serpent with dark, oily scales loomed over the pair. Ephera's eyes widened and she took a step backward but became frozen in place.

Chiki jumped in front of Ephera, ready to strike again. The serpent swayed his long neck, slinking closer. Ephera opened her mouth to scream, but couldn't.

Chiki crouched down, preparing to pounce. Before it could, without warning, a teenage girl with black hair tied messily into a ponytail jumped from behind the horrific creature. The strange girl raised her arms high into the air and, with a shining sword in hand, she sliced through the air, slashing the serpent in two.

Chiki and Ephera stared in wonder at the newcomer.

"You didn't even notice this Shade slithering up here." The teenage girl sheathed her sword. "You two are lucky I was here."

"Thank you." Ephera bowed. "What's your name?"

"Orpheus." The girl held her head high. "And who may you be?"

"My name is Ephera. Your name's really pretty."

"Thanks, I guess." Orpheus turned away from the younger girl. "What are you doing on the outskirts of town late at night? Don't you know that Shades come out at night?"

"It's not night yet." Ephera pointed to the orange orb in the sky. "The sun's still setting."

"It's almost night." Orpheus let out a long sigh and shook her head. "You know what? I don't need this." She walked towards the town, with a scowl on her face and a slightly hunched back.

Ephera tailed behind her like a duckling to its mother.

After several minutes, Orpheus turned around. "Why are you still following me?" She glared at Ephera.

"Well, you seem to know where you're going, and you didn't say anything the whole time. We're in the middle of town you know."

Orpheus looked around, realizing she had escorted Ephera into the town's square. She sighed. "Fine, you know what. I'll help you out. That way you can continue on your own, and I can get back to what I was doing before."

"Oh, if I'm a bother, then it's okay," Ephera said. She tried to escape into the town square, hugging Chiki tighter, but before she could even take three steps, Orpheus grabbed her shoulder.

"Listen. I didn't mean it that way." Orpheus twirled her hair. "You're not a bother. It's really not a problem. I'm not used to company."

"Are you sure?"

"I'm sure. I'll make it up to you. I'll take you to watch the Shooting Stars Festival tonight."

Ephera smiled. "Thank you, Orpheus."

The two explored the town together, visiting various booths of the Shooting Stars Festival. Lanterns brightened the town. Melodies from violins and flutes filled the air. They fished for rubber ducks, popped balloons, and threw bean-bags in buckets, earning themselves stuffed animals and other tacky prizes. Orpheus attempted to strike up a conversation with a lovely young woman, but she stuttered and couldn't find the right words.

Ephera, Orpheus, and Chiki watched a play about two amazing siblings musicians, though, despite Ephera's protests, they left early. Orpheus avoided Ephera's questions as to why. At last, the two made their way to the seaside after dropping off all of their prizes in Orpheus's home.

Orpheus placed a light blue towel on the beach, so that all of them could sit comfortably. The girls buried their feet in the cool sand. Chiki laid in between the girls, its soft fur inviting their hands to pet the ferret.

Ephera began to hum "Ode to Joy," and upon recognizing the familiar tune, Orpheus hummed along as well.

"Your voice is so beautiful." Ephera's eyes shone. "Are you a singer, Orpheus?"

"I"—Orpheus avoided Ephera's gaze of admiration—"*was*."

"What do you mean *was*?"

"Don't you know, Angel? Don't you know what all of us are d—"

Orpheus and Ephera turned around to a piercing screech and saw two pairs of eyes—one red, like rubies, and the other, yellow topazes.

Orpheus pushed Ephera back and drew her sword. She pointed to the creature with the red eyes, and while looking at Chiki said, "C'mon, Guardian. I'll make your job easier and take out the one with yellow eyes. You take out the one with the red eyes."

"Guardian?" Ephera asked.

"Your ferret. Didn't he tell you that he's a Guardian? The magical creatures that protect this land?" Orpheus gripped her sword tightly, waiting for the horse-sized lizard creature to make its first move.

Ephera watched Chiki. It wagged its tail a few times back and forth, and then ran to the creature with red eyes. It jumped high into the night sky, and began charging an energy blast. While it was still mid-air, it fired a beam of light, eradicating the Shade into shadowy dust.

At the same time, both Orpheus and the other creature were circling each other—both waiting for the optimal moment to strike. After several, slow seconds, the Shade charged Orpheus at full speed.

Orpheus inhaled, took a defensive stance, and thrusted her sword into the incoming mass. Its oily body fell to the ground, but it did not fade into dust. Rather, the two pieces rose and struck at Orpheus with their claws.

"Oh no. This is disgusting. It doesn't die." Orpheus wiped blood from her mouth. She stood knees slightly bent, ready to strike.

"Orpheus, be careful!" Ephera yelled. She wanted to do something, but knew she couldn't help. *Your efforts would be useless—You'd only be a burden*. A familiar, but unloving voice echoed in Ephera's head. One half of the Shade turned its attention towards Ephera and lunged at her. She froze. *I can't do anything.* Orpheus tried to chase after it, but the other half blocked her way.

"Don't get in my way." Orpheus slashed the creature. This time she cut its head. Only then did it fade into a shadowy dust.

Meanwhile, Chiki ran in front of Ephera and charged another energy blast, completely eradicating the split off creature.

Ephera fell to her knees, and let out the breath she didn't know she was holding. Orpheus ran over and hugged her. Chiki followed suit and snuggled between the two.

"Are you okay, Ephera?"

Tears fell from Ephera's face. She clutched Orpheus tightly and cried into her arms.

"I can't do anything."

Orpheus stroked her hair. "It's okay. You're young, so we can—"

"No." Ephera broke away from the embrace. "You and Chiki have saved me twice now. If these monsters keep popping up, I want to be able to protect myself and everyone, too."

Orpheus stood up and made direct eye contact with Ephera. "You really don't need to learn how to fight. There are Guardians that will protect you." She tried her best to smile. "And, most importantly, I can protect you."

"You're not making sense, Orpheus," Ephera said. "Why are you not allowing me to learn to fight like you? Why do you want to protect me so much? We were only strangers a few hours ago."

Orpheus's hand twitched. She felt hot, yet cold at the same time. Old memories flooded into her mind as if released from a cage.

A stage filled with blinding lights. Gunshots. A crowd screaming and stampeding. A small girl falling on the piano's keys—the dissonance echoing throughout the room. A young Orpheus clutching the microphone as she watched blood stain the piano. She reached for the small girl's lifeless hands, but was torn away.

"Orpheus, we have to get out of here, it's unsafe." Her teacher throws the girl with neatly braided hair onto her shoulders. Orpheus kicked and screamed as the two run towards the backstage.

"Melody, no! We can't leave my little sister." Soon, darkness engulfs them both. The sounds of police sirens, ambulances, and gunshots are muted—background noises to Orpheus's requiem of tears.

Back in the present, Ephera was screaming. "Orpheus? Orpheus!"

Orpheus sat absolutely still—her eyes were vacant. The ground around her had dark, dusty clouds surrounding her. An oily substance manifested, slowly taking form.

"What's happening?" Ephera backed away slowly.

"Shades are being born," a voice said.

"Who said that?" Ephera turned around, but saw no one except for Chiki. "Chiki? Was that you? Is that telepathy?"

Chiki swished its tail. "Shades are born from negative emotions of humans. And since Orpheus's heart holds such a heavy burden…"

"That mean she's hurting…" Ephera eyes shone like fire. "We have to help."

"That's easier said than done. When people go through this much despair, we Guardians have no choice but to force them to reincarnate. It's not favorable, but—"

Ephera sprinted towards Orpheus. The ferret's words about reincarnation echoed in her head. *Oh, I get it now.* This type of realization would anger many others, perhaps even break them, but all Ephera felt was relief. *So, do I get another try?*

A barrier made of shadowy dust surrounded Orpheus, preventing Ephera from jumping through it.

She pounded and kicked the barrier, screaming Orpheus's name. As she tried to get Orpheus to open up, Shades manifested and attempted to attack Ephera. Chiki fended them off, though the numbers increased exponentially. A few Shades slipped past its defense, and charged to Ephera.

"Ephera, watch out!" Chiki yelled.

Ephera turned away from Orpheus, but instead of running, she placed her feet firmly on the floor and placed her arms at her side. With an unfaltering gaze, she let one of the wolf-like creatures bite her. She refused to budge despite the pain.

"These Shades came from Orpheus, so they're a part of her," Chiki said.

The Shade looked up at Ephera with its crimson eyes.

"Orpheus, please," Ephera pleaded. "I know you don't want to hurt me. Let me help you."

The Shade paused, its jaw loosening on her arm.

"Orpheus," Ephera said. "Please don't do this. This is not what you want."

The Shade, claws raised up to strike, stared into Ephera's eyes. It slowly lowered its claws and edged away.

The barrier opened up.

"I've never seen this happen." Chiki was unable to take its gaze off the two. "Humans never fail to surprise me."

"You can take control, Orpheus." Ephera walked through the weakened barrier. Face-to-face with Orpheus, Ephera took a deep breath. "Orpheus?"

"I'm… sorry…Melody," Orpheus murmured, tears dripping down her face. "It's my fault. It's my fault. It's all my fau—"

"Who's Melody?" Ephera bent down and clutched Orpheus's hand.

"My sister… I couldn't protect her. It's all my fault."

"Your sister? What happened to her?"

"I loved her more than anything. And I cou—"

Ephera flicked Orpheus's forehead. "Stop saying that. You keep saying its your fault, but I bet it wasn't." Ephera puffed out her cheeks as she leaned back and placed both hands on her hips. "I know that you're someone who works really hard and is really nice. Your sister loved you. You're Orpheus. I bet she doesn't blame you at all. If I was her, I wouldn't want my big sister to be sad, so you need to stop blaming yourself." An image of Mr. Hector flashed in Ephera's head. "Sometimes things happen you can't control."

"Ephera." Orpheus slowly moved her head, bringing her eyes up to Ephera's eyes. "You…you didn't have to flick me, you know. That was extremely rude."

Ephera smiled and hugged Orpheus who hugged back. Slowly, the retreating Shades faded away. As the two embraced, shooting stars fell from the night sky. The bright white lights illuminated the dark sky.

Several days later, Orpheus brought Ephera to the train station in town. As they waited for the train to arrive, the two played cards on the train platform.

"Ephera, do you have any sixes?" Orpheus asked. Glancing at Chiki, she cleared her throat. "Chiki, I've always wanted to know this, but can we die in this world?" Orpheus refused to make eye contact with the ferret, and flushed red awaiting an answer.

"No," Chiki replied, "but you can still feel immense pain."

"I see."

"I hope that satisfies your curiosities."

In the distance, bells signaled that the train's approach. It pulled in with great speed, splashing water on the platform and anyone sitting too close. Orpheus was hit with a rather large wave.

"Disgusting," she grumbled as water dripped from her body. Ephera giggled at Orpheus while giving her three cards. Orpheus took them and put them all in her hand.

"It looks like it's time for me to go," Ephera said. "Are you sure you don't want to come with me?"

"I think I'll make a journey to the eastern mountains another day." Orpheus put a hand on her hip. "There are still some things I need to come in terms with."

"I understand." Ephera put her arms out. One last time, the two shared a hug. "Thank you, Orpheus. The days with you were very fun, the most fun I've had in a long time. I'll miss you."

"I'll miss you too, Angel. Thank you for everything. You'll be good by yourself, right?"

"Yes, I will." Ephera giggled. "You know something, Orpheus? When we're both in the normal world again, I'll be older than you."

Orpheus pushed Ephera playfully. "Oh, hush."

When the doors to the train station opened, Ephera entered with Chiki perched on her shoulders. She sat by a window, ready to enjoy the view. As the train departed, Orpheus gave one final wave to Ephera, before turning and walking away, her back straighter and her form stronger, her hair as messy as ever.

"She's going to be alright," Ephera said.

The train glided above the ocean with its tracks submerged in the water. The ocean was clear, allowing Ephera to see the the pink corals, green seaweed, and multi-colored fish. The sea's blue that reflected the white, fluffy clouds from the sky, entranced her. The gentle scene beckoned her to come, to feel the cool water on her skin. It was a sight she had always dreamed of seeing—much better than the illustrations of picture books. Before she knew it, Ephera had dozed off to a slumber full of sweet dreams.

The train travelled for an entire day and entire night. At its last stop, Ephera exited the train and walked outside to see an open plain. It was late afternoon, and the land around her was engulfed in an golden hue. The tall, green grass swayed with the gentle breeze. and the light blue mountains in the distance invited Ephera to come. On the side of the road where a small structure with a sign in curly, bold letters that said "**POST OFFICE,**" a man with a mail carrier hat sat behind a counter with a disorganized pile of letters and envelopes behind him. He was nodding off, and he only snapped awake when he saw Ephera and Chiki.

"You there, Ephera!" He shouted in a volume so loud Ephera was sure that the Normal World could hear him.

"Eek!" Ephera froze. "Yes? How do you know my name?"

"It's on the envelope. Come here. You have two letters." He was gesturing wildly as he shouted for Ephera to come over.

Ephera walked to the stand. The young man handed Ephera two envelopes, and smiled, urging her to open the envelope.

TO: EPHERA   TO: ANGEL (EPHERA)
FROM: MR. HECTOR   FROM: ORPHEUS

"From Mr. Hector and Orpheus?" Ephera felt tears forming in her eyes. "Mr. Post Office Man, how did you get all these letters?"

"When a person writes a letter to another person, it'll show up here," he said, smiling. "If these letter are here, then it means these people specifically requested for them to come to you at the end of your journey."

Ephera tilted her head, her hair falling to one side of her face.

"I've been here for years, Tulip." he kicked back in his seat, placing his legs on the counter. "And honestly, I stopped questioning the magic of this world. Guardians like the one on your shoulder don't tell me anything. By the way, my name's Courway."

Chiki made a sound resembling a snicker.

"Well, thank you for delivering me these letters, Courway." Ephera took Mr. Hector's letter first, and opened the envelope without making a single tear. "How did you know it was me?"

"Magic, Tulip. Everytime I get a letter, I just know who they're for." He pointed two fingers at Ephera and made a *clicking* sound.

The answer was acceptable to Ephera, so she began reading Mr. Hector's letter.

Dear Ephera,

I thought you would like to know that my husband and I have reunited, so there is no need to fight him, oho. If you're reading this letter, it means that your journey is coming to an end, and that you discovered the truth about this world. I apologize for not telling you that this is the afterlife, but I couldn't find it in my heart to tell you. And so, I wish you luck and prosperity in your next life. I shed tears that night when you told me that you never seemed to make your mother happy, and I want you to know you are a child made of sunlight, able to heal the hearts of anyone. My poor, lonely heart was warmed by your presence, and so I wanted to ensure that you would carry on, not blaming yourself for things outside your control.

On your journey, I'm sure that you've helped another troubled heart find peace. Never lose your cheerful disposition Ephera. In your next life, I wish nothing more but for you to live a beautiful, happy, and longer life.

I have been quite charmed by this world, and my husband is also beginning to love this land, as well, so I believe the two of us will remain here. And so, I hope that I will see you again one day, little Ephera.

Mr. Hector

To Angel:

I guess, I must say thank you for everything—like helping me on the night of shooting stars. I'm not good with these letters, but, I wanted to at least tell you that the reason I was so... Uncomfortable around you sometimes. You remind me a lot of my sister, Melody. She is, as you can guess, dead, too. Actually, she's probably alive now—she died years before I did, so I'm sure she reincarnated already. She was the sweetest little girl and the best pianist I ever knew. The two of us, Orpheus and Melody, we were the dream team. We won tons of trophies, and, perhaps someone became envious? Or we were just victims to luck's cruel hand. On the night of our final performance together, Melody was killed. I couldn't do anything to protect her that night. I survived, but those feelings of guilt and inferiority stayed with me up into my own death. That's why I use a sword in this world. I took it up so that I could learn to protect others. I've always been sort of an anime fan, haha. If you don't know what that is, don't worry about it.

I still wish I could see Melody again, and tell her how sorry I am, but you've helped me realize that it really wasn't my fault. I'm still working on convincing myself that there was nothing I could have done, and that Melody would forgive me. Heh, she would have called me a silly goose for worrying about it so much. She was someone who didn't let things get to her, unlike her big sis.

Anyways, this is the end of our letter. I'll be honest, I'm going to miss you. I really hope that in your next life you can live a life that's longer and happier and all that stuff. (Maybe we can even meet again.) You deserve it the most, understand? Also stop apologizing and being sorry. You got kind of better at it, but just in case you forgot. Don't be sorry for things like wanting to spend time with an amazing person like me.

I joke...I'm not that amazing. Maybe. Well, this is goodbye, Ephera.
-Orpheus

Ephera smiled as she hugged the letters close to her heart. "Thank you for delivering these letters to me, Courway."

"It's my job, Tulip. I make sure everyone gets their letters." Courway gave her a wink.

"In that case, do you think I can write some letters in response?"

"Of course." He gave Ephera pieces of paper and assorted colored pens.

By the time the pair reached an inn at the base of the eastern mountains, it was nightfall. The elderly couple in charge welcomed Ephera and Chiki with warm arms and a warm bath. Ephera sank into the tub, soaking herself in the soothing waters. She let out a relaxed sigh as she watched the steam fill the room. After she finished, she noticed that her white dress was replaced with a pastel pink t-shirt and dark blue shorts. When she finished changing, one of the elderly woman came into the room.

"I thought you'd like a new pair of clothes. Something a little more relaxing," the elderly woman explained.

"Oh, thank you so much, Miss…"

"Lyna. Just call me Lyna, dear." She smiled. "Now, I have a question for you. What would you like for dinner?"

"Whatever you have?"

"That won't do, dear. My wife, Flora, can make almost any meal imaginable. Her pride comes from being able to fulfill all of our customers' last requests."

Ephera pondered Lyna's question. She remembered all the hastily prepared meals her mother made with little care. She definitely did not want any of those as her last meals.

"Can I have a bowl of white rice and some fried eggs?"

"Of course. Here, follow me to the dinner table." Lyna beckoned Ephera to follow her.

On a large mahogany table, several people were eating their own meals, be it lobster, ice cream, curry, or cereal. The room was well-lit with lights dangling on the walls. Ephera spotted Chiki sitting on the table, took a seat next to the ferret.

"Welcome back, Ephera, I take it you enjoyed your bath?" Chiki jumped on her lap.

"Yes, I did." Ephera rubbed Chiki's chin with a finger.

Flora came to Ephera and placed a bowl of white rice and a plate of fried eggs in front of Ephera.

"Please, enjoy." She patted both Ephera and Chiki's head.

Ephera smiled. "Thank you for the meal, Flora."

Flora beamed. "You're welcome."

Ephera looked at the meal in front of her. The white rice neatly fit the small, porcelain bowl, resembling snow, and the eggs had perfect, golden centers. When she poked them with her fork, gold rivers flowed on the whites of the egg.

"Chiki, I have a question," Ephera asked.

"Ask away."

"Why did you follow me this entire time?"

"Ah, why do I follow you?" Chiki nuzzled Ephera's cheeks. "I was visiting the mortal world, as my curiosity gets the better of me. Now, I'm magical, so nothing could really hurt me, but a little girl who was buying groceries didn't know that. So, she ran in front of a bus, trying to save me."

"I'm starting to remember now." Ephera mused. "It was a rainy day, and there were a lot of cars. And I saw a little ferret in the street. I was so worried, so I just—" Tears fell on the mahogany table as Ephera clutched her fork. "It was…really scary…"

81

"I'm very sorry, truly. You're here because of my carelessness. That's why I became your companion. Your kindness touched me, and I wanted to keep you safe on your journey to a new life."

"I see. Well, I don't regret what I did." Ephera tried to wipe the tears from her face.

"We're almost at the end of our journey. Eat your meal before it gets cold."

Ephera cut a piece of the egg and ate it with a scoop of rice. As she ate, she cried in silence. Regardless, it was the best meal she ever had.

At sunrise, Ephera set off. In a field of irises illuminated by a lavender hue, Ephera recalled Orpheus's instructions from a few days prior.

"When you make it to the eastern mountains, you need to empty your mind. Be fully ready and content. When that happens, the magic in this world lets you reincarnate." She had patted Ephera on the shoulders. "Don't be scared, Angel."

"Thank you for everything, Orpheus." Ephera smiled.

As she stared at the scenery before her, she remembered the paintings in Mr. Hector's house. "Thank you too, Mr. Hector."

Ephera gazed at the sun barely peeking over the blue mountains that reached for the morning sky.

"Whenever you're ready." Chiki jumped on Ephera's shoulders. "Let the wind take you."

"Okay." Ephera closed her eyes, as the gentle breeze blew. She felt like a leaf, flying through the air. "I know where I am, and even though I wish I had more time, I'm glad I'm here."

"Any last questions?" Chiki asked.

"I have one." Ephera, with eyes still closed, held up one finger. "What's beyond the sky?"

"Ah. Beyond the sky, your new life awaits. New experiences. New people. New dreams."

"I can't wait." Ephera looked up towards the sky. "Thank you, Chiki. You kept me and everyone safe."

"It's my job as a Guardian, after all." Chiki jumped off Ephera and was silent for a few seconds. "Ah, your time is drawing near. You will reincarnate soon."

Ephera opened her eyes and looked at her transparent hands. Tears fell on the petals of the irises below. "I'm going to miss everyone, but I also really want to live life again. I want one that's better."

"It's what everyone deserves." Chiki turned its head away, unable to look at Ephera. "No crying," Chiki whispered, mostly to itself.

Ephera wiped the tears from her face, pumped her fists, and smiled.

"I'll see you again, one day. But, hopefully it's not too soon. Bye, Chiki."

"Goodbye, Ephera. May your light always shine on others." Chiki said as it turned its head back to where Ephera was standing. Ephera, with eyes closed once again, gave one last wave as she faded away in the light of the rising sun.

Lillies grow for when certain lights die,
Their petals soothe the departed's cries,
Her journey, sunset to sunrise, ends,
In a path opposite of the sun,
When dawn comes, her new life has begun.

WHO TAKES CARE OF THE UNFORTUNATE?
By Kristy Diep

Men of status,
Created from days,
Spilled onto nights,
In shadows of a supreme,
Hid behind figures of average beings,
Blinded,
By things of much less value,
Fortune,
Power.

Reached out,
Took a step,
Believed,
Help was on the way,
Patient,
They were almost destined,
The soft touch of potential,
That had barely been caressed,
Has vanished into oblivion.

Where those of authority were cherished,
Taken care of,
Appreciated.

Pull back the curtains,
Reveal the truth,
Dominance of aspiration,
Those who sought to be,
In control,
Best of the best,
All was just a test,

Who will pass?
Exceeds who shall fail,
Survival of the evil,
Death of the miserable,
Fall of our system,
Broken,
For those who are unfortunate,
Are overlooked,
Are forgotten.

MESSLETTERS
By Hien Phan

4.

Here lies the wasteland of memories
I pick up the stars, glowing at my fingertips
They stand to wait, they wait to stand
Upon my call, they glow like candle-lights
I pick one and ask her to look for my love
In the meantime, I recall my story

1.

Once upon-a-time, twice upon-a-time
No matter how many upon-a-times it takes
Never forget, I shall never forget your smile
These wings of mercy, I pray, take me by your side
Swift and quick; they only came the first time
(No matter how much I called)
Ah, I remember the first time
We danced at the edge of the water,
Ocean, we met, your name I loved
What form does a God take when they become human?
I asked, though I knew the answer
My love, keep this memory close to my heart

2.

Thrice upon-a-time, half a dozen upon-a-time
Never ending upon-a-times, I know my love
Our story gives color, love and kindness
Bright words, pretty language, love letters
I ask for a letter back now; none return
(No matter how much I call)
I reach for your hand, couple it with a ring
I breathe your name, ask you to breathe mine
We laugh at the altar, embrace joyously
Upon which we sing, like a pair of lovebirds
I asked that you look up at the night sky

Those stars, they shine for you! My love, oh so beautiful
They shine for you, gleam, and I cannot break my gaze away
Your eyes dazzle and your voice, like bells
Captivate me, my love, keep me close

3.

A dozen upon-a-times, a score upon-a-time
All of these upon-a-times, I cannot forget
My sorrow reaches for the skies
Fingers entangling amongst the constellations
I miss you, I call out for you; you do not answer
(No matter how much I call)
From your cold body comes a star so bright
I fail to see anyone else and fall to my knees
My hands, my tears, they flow, they grasp
Nothing, they—nothing, they—they—
I plead—God, are you there? please, return my love
But alas, no matter how much I call
No answer and I look up to see
Two bright lights approaching me
Is that you, God? I beg, and with an impact
The vehicle, driver and I, our hearts stop at once
And then I wake up here, my love
In this wasteland of memories

5.

I pick up the stars, glowing at my fingertips
They stand to wait, they wait to stand
Upon my call, they glow like candle-lights
I look up and see you, with a star in your arms
And we embrace, in this constellation of dreams

Karyōbinga

By Krista Phanpraphou

based on the surimono, 1820-1833 by Katsushika Hokusai

Listen to this peaceful melody
Feel the music embrace your soul,
feel yourself being swallowed in
Along within the Darkness lies the dim Light
Jeweled specks shine through this dark alleyway,
guiding you towards the path of the right
Listen to this peaceful melody,
and visualize a gentle black feather
Imagine yourself touching it,
enjoy the smooth patterns
traditional crimson and ebony
Now as she plays the God's flute, let her rise
Let her rise from her deep slumber
Let her rise from the depths of human dreams
Let her rise from the feeding of souls
who dearly enjoy this beautiful song of hers
Silent in complete darkness,
look around and open your eyes
See yourself living in this reality
And notice this alluring melody once again

Let her be your wings,
let her music be within you
For I am Karyōbinga.

BY THE PHONE BOOTH

By Johnson Nguyen

You're gone, somewhere far away,
but hopefully I'll see you again, maybe another day.
If I ever do, I would let go of the past
and spend time with you, like every moment was its last.
I'd work on the mistakes that scarred me and you;
I'd try to make things better between us two.
That will never happen I know that's the truth,
I'll still be here, by the phone booth, waiting for you.
I've gone a long way trying to find where you are,
but I'm just wasting my time because I'm lost in the stars.
Oh, all the possibilities we could've been,
But now my worn out heart is hurting within.
And the days when I lie on my bed,
All the thoughts I'm thinking just hurt my head.
I'd do anything to see you I wouldn't restrain,
I'd travel a long journey just to end this pain.
I know it won't happen, but what else can I do
Besides stand here by the phone booth, still in love with you.

NAVIGATION
By April Trinh

humans are not made to settle—
we march to our gentle, sloping heartbeat
into another sky—
or so You told me when we
sat under our pocket of stars
on our balcony overlooking the sea.

we have no destination, but we will settle
for that endless sea—
where half of the stars
sink—but You remain fixed in the sky
and You told me that we
would be one, with the sea's heartbeat.

under the darkened sky,
i can only hear my heartbeat—
we had no compass, but we would settle
with our map made of stars—
i no longer know our destination, but we
still sink deeper into this sea.

the light sunken in the sea
contains the life of long dead stars—
or so You told me when we
made an oath under a peachy sky
with the ephemeral clouds that settled
under the hill, close to the earth's heartbeat.
our journey was halted by the stormy sea;
with my heartbeat
like the flickering star,
with Your eyes dark against the sky,

and i knew that we
were not made to settle.

i know that we
were not made to be eternal, but the sea
in its infinity, the stars
in the inky sky
in its eternity, settle
in our love, Your heartbeat.

My heartbeat and the sea
carries Us far and We
become stars—

A NIGHT TO REMEMBER
By Kimberly Nguyen

BRIDGET SQUINTED AT THE beam of sunlight that had managed to squeeze through a crack between the lavender drapes. She rolled onto her back and stretched her arms above her head with a loud groan before wincing at the sharp pain in her right temple. A high-pitched ringing echoed in her ear, intensifying the pain. She grabbed her head. As she rubbed her forehead, her hand brushed off a yellow post-it note that fluttered to the floor.

Momentarily forgetting about the pounding in her head, Bridget picked up the note, but it was too dark to read what was written on it. She set it on couch.

Pulling herself up, she opened her eyes. *I must have fallen asleep on the couch again.* The blurred outline of the rectangular glass coffee table came into focus in front of her.

I need more light. She glanced across the room at the bay window. She hadn't taken but two steps before her bare feet squished onto a wet spot on the area rug under the coffee table. Ignoring the strange wetness, she went to the window and flung open the curtains permitting sunshine to stream in.

She squinted and went back to the area rug. Something had soaked into the dense fabric, creating a musty smell that filled the room. Bridget stared at the dark stain on the paisley pattern, her eyes still adjusting to the brightness of the daylight. A sharp pang resonated in her temple again. *The post-it note. What was written on it?*

She examined the letters scribbled on it in black pen:

Find Me: 2041B2ND

It must be one of the girls playing a joke on me. Making herself comfortable back on the couch, Bridget propped her feet up on the coffee table. She mentally rehearsed yesterday's events. She had returned to the apartment after her part-time job at the diner around 6 o'clock, but everything after that was a blur. She stared at the yellow note in her hand. *What had happened last night?*

The sound of keys unlocking the front door broke the silence. Janet and Leni's voices echoed in from the hallway. Janet entered the living room, dressed in her beige winter coat, a red plaid scarf wrapped around her neck.

"What is that smell?" Janet shoved Bridget's feet off the coffee table. "It smells like you killed something in here."

Bridget braced herself for a scolding. Unlike her, Janet was adamant in having the apartment looking like a furniture store display: everything in its place, and nothing out of place. *Better not let Janet know I might have spilled something on the rug.*

Leni entered the living room in her oversized gray sweater and black leggings. "Were you and Maya alright here alone last night? No fighting right?" Her eyes sparkled like stars as she smiled.

"Hey—uh—do you know what happened last night?" Bridget rubbed the back of her neck.

"We were helping Leni's sister move into her new apartment last night, remember?" Janet placed the decorative pillows back into their place on the couch. "That smell is awful. I'm opening the windows."

"Are you alright, Bridget?" Leni asked. She poured herself a cup of coffee in the kitchen. "You look exhausted."

"I...I think so?" Bridget looked at the post-it note in her hand.

"What's the deal with the post-it?" Janet placed her hands on her hips and leaned to look at Bridget's hand.

"I found this on my forehead this morning," Bridget said. "I thought it was from one of you."

Leni returned from the kitchen with the cup of coffee. She looked at Janet. "Wasn't us." She took a seat on the couch next to Bridget. "What does it say?"

Bridget handed the post-it to Leni. "Looks like some kind of code."

"Well, did you ask Maya? She was the one home with you last ni—" Janet stared at the scarlet stain on the rug. "What is that?" She glared at Bridget.

"It was Maya." Bridget blurted out the words before she could stop them. *Sorry Maya.*

"What did she spill? It smells horrible." Janet grabbed a dark rag from the kitchen and scrubbed at the stain. "Where is Maya?"

"She was gone when I woke up."

"Hey, isn't this our apartment number?" Leni pointed to the first three digits on the post-it note.

"It is." Bridget moved closer to Leni on the couch.

After a failed attempt to get the stain out, Janet tossed the rag into the laundry basket and joined Bridget and Leni on the couch. "Let me see." She grabbed the post-it note from Leni's hand. She held the post-it up to her face. "Weren't the bedrooms labeled when we first moved in here?"

"They were, weren't they?" Bridget glanced toward the hallway that led to the bedrooms. "One B....Wasn't that Maya's room?"

"Let's check it out." Leni poked Bridget's arm with a manicured finger.

"We shouldn't be going through her room when she's not home," Janet said, but it was too late, Bridget and Leni were already at Maya's bedroom door. Janet sighed and said, "Just like children." She stood up and followed behind them.

Bridget stared at the wooden plaque that hung from a twine string on the door. Maya's name was etched into the plaque. A high pitched ring exploded in Bridget's ears, causing her to lose her balance and grab the doorframe. She closed her eyes as the pain in her temple emerged from its hiding spot in the back of her mind. An image of Maya appeared. She wore her favorite t-shirt and black shorts and stumbled backward down the hallway. Her shoulder-length brown curls bounced as she shook her head. Tears streamed down her cheeks. She was screaming something, but Bridget couldn't hear anything over the ringing in her ears.

"Hey, you okay Bridge?" Janet placed a hand on Bridget's shoulder.

"Yeah." The image of Maya faded away, replaced by the image of the bedroom door in front of her. The ringing stopped. "Let's go in, yes?"

Leni opened the door. Maya's bedroom was in chaos. The blankets and pillows that were usually neatly placed on the bed by the wall were thrown askew on the floor. Clothes hung halfway out of the dresser drawers as if they had tried to jump out but didn't quite make it. Maya's desk by the door was the only thing seemingly untouched.

How did this happen? Bridget thought.

"Hey look." Janet pointed to a post-it note on the second drawer of the desk. The note was yellow like the first and on it, in the same black ink, was scribbled:

2ND

"Another part of the code," Bridget said. She pulled open the drawer. Inside was empty except for another post-it note with the word:

Fridge

"There's ano—" Bridget turned around to show Janet and Leni but they had already left the room. Bridget walked into the hallway and followed Leni into the kitchen. There were two untouched plates of pasta neatly placed on the small oak table that sat in the center of the kitchen. A half-drunk glass of red wine rested on the table. Some of the wine had spilled onto the table, as if someone had abandoned the glass in a hurry.

The ringing started again and Bridget stared at the plates on the table. Her vision blurred and for a moment everything seemed dark. Bridget's vision cleared and she could see Maya again. This time she was standing by the table with a plate of pasta in her hand. Bridget could see the steam floating from the plate. Maya placed the plate down on the table and took a sip from her glass of wine, leaving a faint lipstick stain on the glass. She smiled at Bridget as she took a seat at the table.

Maya began to talk, her eyes lighting up as she told her story, but what escaped her lips was muffled. Bridget strained to hear what Maya said but to no avail. *"I can't hear you,"* Bridget said. Maya's smile faded into a concerned line. She reached her hand out to Bridget, only to quickly pull it back.

Bridget's vision blurred. The pounding in her temple intensified. *What happened to Maya? What really happened last night?* Bridget shook her head. She was facing Maya again, but this time Maya was screaming at her. She watched as Maya waved her hands in the air in angry gestures. *What was she upset about now?*

Bridget opened her eyes. Janet and Leni were standing in front of the refrigerator. Leni had pulled open the doors and was digging through its contents while Janet ran her fingers up and along the sides of the refrigerator. Bridget joined them. She pulled a chair from the table and climbed onto it. She scanned the top of the refrigerator and noticed another yellow post-it note and a key.

"I think I found something." Bridget climbed down from the chair and showed her findings to her roommates. The paper simply read a single word:

Open

Janet picked up the key. "It looks like our house key."

"But look." Leni pointed to the number etched into the key. "It says 205."

"The apartment next door? That place has been vacant for months." Bridget stared at the post-it note.

"Why would we have a key?" Janet asked.

"Well there's only one way to find out." Leni picked up the key between two fingers and before anyone could stop her, was out the front door.

"Hurry, let's follow her." Janet grabbed Bridget by the wrist and pulled her out the door.

Leni was struggling with the key at the other apartment. Seeing Leni, Janet released Bridget's wrist and went to help her.

The three girls were met with the smell of cleaning supplies as the door swung open. The apartment was completely empty.

"I didn't know the landlady was capable of keeping anything this clean," Leni said, looking at the spotless white tiles that covered the floors.

"I don't think this is a good idea." Bridget backed into the hallway.

"We've gotten this far, might as well find out where this leads us," Janet said, leading the way into the apartment, followed by Leni.

Bridget could hear their voices from the hallway. Leni was going on about some boyfriend of hers who owned a house with the same tile flooring. *What should I do? There could be a serial killer in there for all they know. And Maya? Where is she? Why do I keep seeing her?* Bridget thought.

Leni's scream echoed into the hallway, bringing Bridget back from her thoughts. Bridget could feel the pit of her stomach tighten. Taking a deep breath, she ran into the apartment. Following the sound of Leni's sobs, Bridget made her way into one of the back bedrooms of the apartment. Leni stood by Janet's side, her face turned into Janet's shoulder. Janet pat her back as Leni sobbed.

"Hey what's going—" She paused when she saw the mass that was sprawled out on the floor. Maya was lying on her back. She was still wearing the same t-shirt and shorts from Bridget's vision. Against the pale tiles of the floor, a crimson puddle of liquid formed from under Maya's body.

"H-how?" Bridget struggled to find words as she stared at Maya's body laid out on the floor. Bridget felt her stomach churn as she saw the dark bruise on Maya's forehead.

The sharp pain at her temple returned. This time Bridget could see Maya. She was walking into the living room with a glass of wine in her hand. Bridget could feel a sudden rage build in her chest and all she could think about was hurting Maya. She tried to push the thought away but it kept returning. She wanted Maya to hurt that way she was hurting. Bridget approached Maya who stood by the coffee table and in one swift movement, she shoved Maya. The glass of wine wobbled as it left her grasp, flinging red droplets onto the table. Bridget flinched as Maya's head hit the table in an ear splitting crack.

Bridget dropped to the floor screaming. She clutched her head between her hands. *Why is this happening? Why me? What did I ever do to deserve this?* Panic raced through her mind.

"Bridge, Bridge. What's happening?" Janet knelt by Bridget and put her hand on Bridget's shoulder.

Startled, Leni stood where she was, tears still streaming down her face.

"Listen to me," Janet said. "It's going to be okay. We'll call the police and—"

Bridget grabbed Janet's arm before she could finish. "It's my fault," Bridget said through sobs.

"Why would you blame yourself for this?" Janet asked.

"It's my fault," Bridget repeated. "I-I-I," she gasped for air between sobs. "It was an accident."

Leni crouched next to Janet. "Do you mean...*you* did this?"

Bridget nodded her head. "It was an accident. I didn't mean to...all I did was push her."

"Bridge," Janet said, "calm down and tell us what happened."

"Last night, Maya accused me of stealing her stuff...She's always had it out for me, ever since she moved in." Bridget wiped her face with the back of her hand. "We fought...and...and...Oh, Janet, all I did was give her a little push."

Bridget pulled her legs up to her chest. "She hit her head on the coffee table. I-I tried to stop the bleeding but there was too much blood. I was so scared."

"No. No, this isn't happening. This can't be rea—" Leni rushed out of the room, sobbing.

"Hey, it's not your fault. It was an accident. Anyone could see that." Janet patted Bridget's back. "Now calm down, okay? You know that I have to call the police now, right?"

Janet stood up and pulled her cell phone from her pocket, walking into the hallway. Bridget followed her out.

"Hello? Hi, I would like to report a mur—" Bridget clamped her hand over Janet's mouth and pulled her by the waist back into the bedroom.

"I'm sorry Janet. I can't let you do this," Bridget whispered into Janet's ear as she slammed the door shut and locked it.

THAT EMBRACE
By Thanh Nguyen

Sometimes all you need is a hug
from someone you love,
Nothing more, just a hug.
A simple hug that can light up a soul,
And warm an empty heart.
It is a beauty, it is forever.
It is that moment when you realize
you are not alone,
And for that reason,
a dead and lonely road
Has become a blooming garden.

REBIRTH
By Thanh Nguyen

Death
Dark, Sad
Dying, Fading, Passing
Ghost, Spirit, Human, Creature
Living, Growing, Breathing, Flourishing
Bright, Happy
Life

BITE

By Jennifer Ho

The drops of rain batters his already wet clothes,
He lets out a weary sigh.
He is not able to protect his fragile possessions,
For he is not even able to protect himself,
From the stingy cold of New York City.

Crowds of people pass by him,
Along with the aromatic smell of their grub,
A little girl trails away from her father,
Handing the poor man her half eaten sandwich,
With an apology that she was not able to do more.

The man smiles despite his weakness,
Gifting her his golden military pin
His only meaningful belonging.
The little girl exclaims her delight
Before she waves goodbye.
The man then takes a bite of the sandwich—

his very last bite.

A LONE RED
By HongAnh Nguyen

A red flower, red leaf.
Red car, red jeep.
Red umbrella, standing in the crowd.
Red balloon, high in the clouds.
Red rose, in your hand.
One that'll never be held again.
Red love, redder than red,
Deeper than love, darker than red.
A love meant for you.
A love that was true.
A love on a thread,
A love that is dead.

WITH TIME
By Michelle Nguyen

THERE ARE TIMES WHEN you'd think the bad parts are endless but someone or something crosses your path and suddenly even the trees start to matter. This is a story of a young girl who loved the forest and a young boy who adored the clouds.

Amanda spent most of her free time in the woods five minutes from her house. She was in the sixth grade. She did her homework by sunlight, sitting on one of the branches of her favorite tree. After school, she'd run home to her mother who packed her snacks, and with that in hand, Amanda walked to her second home.

Kyle watched her scramble out of the classroom before everyone else. He knew where she was headed to everyday. It was no mystery; Amanda wrote about what she saw in the woods in her daily journals. When called upon to share, she even encouraged classmates to visit the therapeutic place. She'd talk passionately, sometimes with her clear brown eyes glistening as each word rolled off her tongue. All her words correlated to her time in the forest and frankly, she didn't care if people were growing tired of her stories.

Kyle had contemplated her invitations for some time but decided the clouds wouldn't look very pretty beneath the thick canopies. The boy was an aspiring artist, coming from a wealthy family that supplied him with only the best paint and sketchbooks. On both good and bad days, he found himself sitting on the balcony of his bedroom gazing at the forever summer skies of Arizona.

Amanda found him sitting under a scarce tree half an hour before the first school bell was to ring. Kyle was peeking through the gaps between leaves, making tiny marks and erasing every now and then. Something about the way he was squinting and muttering under his breath as he constantly looked up to the sky and down to his lap made her feel unwelcome; she didn't think it was right to disturb such concentration. Even still, she didn't feel that she needed to leave. She ducked behind a tree trunk and slid down until her bottom reached the roots. She then pulled out her breakfast and looked up to the sky, trying to grasp what Kyle had been looking at.

Kyle glanced at the watch on his wrist and noted there were only ten minutes remaining before the start of school. He glanced at his lap and saw another sketch of the day's clouds and smiled to himself. Packing up, he walked out of the forest and decided that his first visit was surely memorable. He captured the spread of the branches and leaves. As he thought about what he was going to do after school, he spotted a blonde ponytail resting behind a trunk. It must be Amanda, he thought to himself.

"Thank you," Kyle said. The forest seemed to echo his words and make them sound twice as loud.

Amanda stirred to her feet, her sun kissed cheeks burned at the sound of his voice. She knew it was just the two of them but half expected him to not talk to her. She balanced herself on tree roots still hidden as she called out, "For what?"

"Taking me here."

Amanda smiled to herself as she heard the crunch of dried leaves under Kyle's fading footsteps.

Kyle came back the next day at around the same time with a sketchbook and packed breakfast and lunch for two. As did Amanda, with two sleeping bags and pillows.

It was a sunny Saturday with a light wind and a sky so blue it made everything below it look smaller. Amanda had already set up the sleeping bags and pillows down at a spot where the two could avoid sunlight shining in their eyes. That day she brought with her many paper doilies from her mother's cupboard of everything tea related. She thought a drawing at the center of the paper would look lovely as a gift to her mother for stealing the doilies. Kyle came a bit later on his bike with multiple brown bags in its basket and four juice boxes.

The day before, after discussing their picnic plans, the two sat together at the farthest table from the playground.

Kyle had asked, "Do you ever get hungry in the forest? Or do you pack yourself food every time you come?"

"I don't really get hungry. My mom packs me food anytime I leave the house."

"Have you ever gotten your food stolen by an animal?"

Amanda smiled at her new friend. "No, but my orange juice once leaked out of my paper bag. I cried."

Kyle laughed so hard at this, the crinkles at the corners of his eyes deepened. His pale cheeks grew rosy as a smile stretched across his face. After a moment, he asked, "Do you like orange juice that much?"

"I love orange juice."

Later that night, he made sure to go to the market with his father to stock up on orange juice boxes.

Kyle made his way over to Amanda sitting on her blue sleeping bag and set the packed food down between them. Neither exchanged a word before he leaned over and showed her how to draw wildflowers. And after she blushed looking at the end result of her own sketch, Kyle tore out his favorite page in his sketchbook and handed it to her.

By the end of the day, an hour before the sun was to set, as Amanda had said, the two had used up all of the paper doilies. Each had a drawing of something related to nature. They rolled up the sleeping bags and pillows and gathered up their trash. Kyle's mother had made them spaghetti, which Amanda greatly enjoyed with her juice.

It was nearly dark by the time they stepped outside of the safe environment that was the forest and exchanged their goodbyes before parting ways.

One day, while flipping through her best friend's artwork, Amanda realized Kyle had been drawing fewer and fewer clouds every day.

"Kyle," she asked, "why have you stopped drawing the clouds so often?"

"I realized there was more to my life than just drifting away."

Amanda stared at his naturally pale face for five seconds, the mechanisms in her brain trying to process his words. He always spoke with such grace that confused her little mind. Eventually, like most times, she looked away as did he; neither knew if they wanted to be able to understand each other so well.

However, just this once, Kyle turned his head back towards the girl with flowers intertwined in her hair and said, "Thank you."

DEMONS DISGUISED AS SOLDIERS, A WWI POEM

By Kristen Nguyen

Time and time again I find myself here
Why must the war go on?
Is God near?

Let me speak to Him, for I have questions
People perish before me every day
I am a lowly witness of Death's handiwork
It causes me great dismay.

Why, God?
Men risking their lives every day in the trenches
Shot down, their bodies twisting and turning like wrenches
Demons disguised as soldiers, taking their opponents out
With reckless abandon, one by one

Their fierce yet anguished cries are heard all throughout
Acting as a warning to all who try to stop them.

Struggling to maintain their sanity
The only thing that keeps them going is their families
And the thought of freedom.

The Lord looks down at them, whispering words of hope
"Do not fret; The war will be over soon."

TO THE YOUNG MAN IN THIS CAFÉ
By Kimberly Nguyen

To the young man seated across the café:
I couldn't help but notice your discomfort with the glances from others in your
direction.
It scares me how quick people are to judge.
They say your appearance tells much about you but from where I stand,
Your actions tell me much more.

It wasn't your dirty white t-shirt that caught my attention.
It was your kindness in holding open the door for that elderly woman on your way
in.
Your tattered jeans tell less of a story than your smile and "Good morning"
As you passed my table.

The faded, worn down shoes that rested on your feet were nothing compared to
the patience you showed to the new cashier struggling to get your change.
Do not be shamed by those dirty glances across the room.
Know that there is at least one person here that sees more than your clothing.

COOPED UP
By Vy Ngo

My alarm clock screams
As I try to reach for it.
Sunlight slowly shines across my face
As the morning birds chirp
It is 8 AM on a Saturday.
I roll around on my bed,
Reluctant to get up.
For I want to stay cooped up.
My blanket is big,
Cozy, and warm.
It coats my entire body
And protects me
From the cold California weather.
I nuzzle against the soft, thick fabric.
It's been ten minutes; I still haven't gotten up,
For I want to stay cooped up.
I stare up at the white ceiling,
I glance at my backpack,
I have work to get done.
But it's a Saturday,
And I want to stay cooped up.
I look at the clock.
Oh no… it's almost noon.

IN ONLY FIVE MINUTES
By Daniela Solano

Monday, April 5, 2015 3:00 P.M.

LIKE ANY NORMAL DAY, the birds chirped, the leaves of the maple trees swayed with the wind, and Elle and Jacob sat on the swing set that never seemed to change even through the harshest rainstorms and bitter cold afternoons. It wasn't until this day that the rust became visible to the eyes of those who had been blind to the gradual damage.

Monday, April 5, 2015 3:10 P.M.

"What do you want to study once we graduate?" Jacob said as he kicked the wood chips under his red sneakers.

Elle, entranced by the way the sunlight illuminated Jacob's light brown hair and pale face, couldn't hear a word he said.

"Elle?" Jacob said.

"Huh? Oh, sorry," Elle said, trying to hide her flushed cheeks.

"I asked what you wanted to study after we graduate high school," he replied.

"Oh, I don't know," she said. "A doctor."

"A doctor? You can't stand Biology class and you're always drawing."

"So? My drawings don't mean anything." Elle looked down. "It's not like I can do that for a living."

"Weren't you ever told that you should do something that you enjoy?" Jacob asked.

"You know how my parents are.. How could I ever become an artist? I mean, I'm not even good enough," Elle said as she shifted her gaze toward the white puffy clouds. "Besides, they're just stupid sketches."

"Your drawings are good. Even the art teacher said so when you won the city watercolor contest last year," Jacob said. "Besides, didn't you get accepted for the art internship in New York? Why did you join if you knew that you couldn't be an artist, huh?

Elle sighed. "You're right, but I just can't face my parents…Can you help me? What are you doing on Saturday?"

I'm probably just going to stay home and do homework. Why? Were you going to ask me out?" Jacob playfully kicked her swing.

"Pfft, you wish," she said, trying to keep cool even though her cheeks did otherwise.

"Who knows, maybe I do." He smiled. "Anyways, I'll see ya later." Jacob hopped off the swing, leaving it behind, along with Elle's opportunity to hang out with him. She knew that she couldn't let any more chances slip away. She needed to find a way to show him how she really felt. She just needed to find out how to tell him.

3:30 P.M.

"Mom, I'm home." Elle ran up the stairs into her bedroom. After slamming the door, she plopped onto her bed. She let herself fall into the comforter's warm embrace. The lingering thoughts on how to confess her feelings to Jacob circled through her mind. She groaned and tried to get up from her bed, remembering she still had tons of homework to finish.

After what felt like an eternity of Calculus homework, she couldn't help but daydream about how she was going to tell Jacob. That's when she knew she had to do research. After an hour, she came across the perfect online article. "How to find out if a guy likes you in three simple steps."

"Step 1: locate your target. Make sure he's the one. Be realistic. If he's out of your league, don't even bother."

"Check, that's one down," Elle said.

"Step 2: Make sure you already talk to this person and have a comfortable relationship with them. If not, the last step will be difficult."

"Check again? Man I'm good at this." She patted herself on the back.

"Step 3: This is the trickiest part. Trick him. Tell him you are unavailable and make him do the chasing."

"Woah, I've never thought of that." She shut her computer down. "I guess this will have to do."

7:02 PM

Elle didn't know how Jacob would react. She wanted a fairy tale. The girl likes the boy, the boy likes her back, and he won't give her up. Sadly, this wasn't a fairy tale. She paced back and forth in the nightgown that Jacob had given her. Each step she took felt like her heart was going to rip out of her chest. After much pacing, Elle dialed Jacob's phone number and sat on the edge of her bed.

7:05 P.M.

"Hello?" a groaning voice said through the line.

"Hey, Jacob, you busy?" Elle asked.

"Well, I was doing calculus homework. What's up?"

"Really, well it sounded like you were sleeping to me."

"Okay, so I was dozing off. I mean, how can't I?" Jacob asked. "Too much studying."

"Well, sorry to wake you but I have good news," she said, grasping onto the cord for dear life.

"Really, well what are you waiting for? Tell me," Jacob said, scribbling a few words onto a post-it note.

Hearing his voice made Elle regret ever calling him, but there was no going back now.

"Well, I wanted to tell you that we won't be able to hang out as much anymore because I have a boyfriend now," Elle said, releasing a huge weight off her shoulders. She finally felt like she could breathe again.

Jacob stopped writing. A growing silence broke with the sound of Jacob's voice.

"Well congratulations, I guess. Listen, I - I have to go. See you tomorrow." Jacob slammed his phone.

"Jacob wait," Elle blurted, but he had already hung up. Elle, still holding her phone to her face, felt warm tears roll down her flushed cheeks.

"Would you like to go out with me, Elle?" Jacob read the post-it note over and over, in a futile attempt to keep tears from forming in his eyes. He wasn't as strong as he thought he was. Tears rolled down his face. Taking the post-it note, he crumpled it tightly in his hand and threw it at the floor. Gritting his teeth, he began to sob.

"I just want her to be happy."

WHAT HAPPENS?
By Vylan Tran

I look at you, wondering why me?
Why do you love me?
It makes me happy that we're in love
But I'm starting to get worried.
What happens if…
I'm not the girl that you wanted me to be,
That I'll get too attached.
That I'm too much of a drama queen.
What happens if…
You don't love me anymore,
Think I'm worthless.
What if you cheat on me,
Start to hate me,
Break up with me.
What happens if…
Just what will happen?

Well, it did.
You broke up with me,
Blamed me for everything.
I never thought you'd do that.
Breaking me with words again and again.
Saying things just to make me cry.
You don't care if you break my heart.
What did I do wrong?
I was being myself.
Being me.

You say you don't love me anymore.
Why did you lie?
You said you have lust for me.
Asking me why'd I even waste my time with you
Why did I think that we had a chance?
You were glad we broke up.
How could you say that?
I didn't know you hated me that much.
You will never understand,
How much you really hurt me.

TRUST IN ME

By Emily Tran

When I met her
My mind said no
You have school to worry about
You have family to worry about
You have church to worry about
Don't you dare
You'll only break her
Hurt her
Bruise her
Suffocate her
When I met her again
I couldn't stop thinking about her
My heart pushed through my chest
You'll be good to her
You want her
You need her
Trust me you can only do good by her
She'll make you a better person
It said
She'll hold you
It said
She wants you
It said
You love her
It told me
I cross my heart and hope to die
If I ever do something
To keep her from being mine
I'm trusting my heart
I hope you do too
Because I swear that I'll love you
All the way through

FIGHTING FOR WHAT'S INSIDE
By Alvin Nguyen

Love is a feeling that can only be found inside
A warm feeling that you can't elsewhere find
A feeling so powerful, it can change the stubborn
Love within is something to savor,
and something to aim for

If I were to fight for another's love,
I would cross the sky
Without fear of tears or lasting scars
If I were to fail, don't be disappointed
And if I go, please don't cry—
know that I have tried

Tied to that powerful feeling
I feel like it's controlling me
I might need help to heal
To show to me, to reveal
that without it, I am still alive
Because even if I strive for another's love
To not find it, does not mean that I will die

A 5 LETTER WORD
By Thanchau Chu

Trust.
How can I trust you
When I can't read what's on your mind
And can only guess
As I look at you from behind.
How can I trust you
When you've chosen me
Out of a zillion better people
That everyone else doesn't see.
How can I trust you
When I can't bear to leave you
Because that's just how much I love you
But I can't get myself to tell you.
Trust is a string, a red string, that never tears.
But ours,
How can I tape this string together
This string that's already been torn for hours.

SEASONS

By Phuong Traceyle

Spring—rise of new life
Buds on trees and babies born,
Where the weather warms

Creatures awaken
From their deep hibernation
Searching for their prey.

Buds grow to blossoms
Blooming from branches of trees
No longer naked.

Grass sprouts everywhere,
Bees pollinate for honey,
Butterflies flutter.

Sizzling summer,
Animals need to hydrate,
The days are lively.

The heat beats us down
We suffer, seek ice water
Cool and refreshing

The plants and flowers,
Fully grown to be consumed,
And for cool shelter

Through Autumn or fall,
The weather begins to chill
Leaves change their color

Like bears and owls,
some animals eat a lot,
preparing slumber.

Leaves start to brittle,
Red, orange, gold, and brown
They fall to the ground

Winter is freezing,
All livings keep themselves warm,
Everything's naked.

Some places have snow
Beautiful snowflakes fall down
Forming snow blankets.

FORGIVENESS
By Karen Phung

Suddenly, suddenly…
It is but a blurry memory
Faces scream and cry of great sorrow
Little do they know I bid them goodbye tomorrow,

Forgive me God for my use of profanity
Forgive me Lord for a life creating felonies
Unable to face the problems that I dread,
I rid of the pain that overwhelm my head.

Consumed in deep waves, sink to the floor
I forget about the torment that left my body sore
A small glance to the sky above
I say goodbye to the ones I love

Begging, begging, begging for forgiveness
Forgive me God it is only for my happiness
Apologies to you as I cannot be forgiven
I cut out the chance for another day to live.

BREAKING THE ICE

By Daniela Solano

CHARACTERS

SPORTSCASTER 1 JOHN BROWN: adult male,
SPORTSCASTER 2 SUSAN WALKER: adult female
TINA DAVIS: 17 years old, tall, pristine, focused on academics, hardworking, popular
JASON WILLIAMS: 17 years old, short, scrawny, nerdy, intelligent
AMANDA: 17 years old, TINA's best friend

FADE IN:
INT. TELEVISION STUDIO
JOHN and **SUSAN** are seated behind a counter in a news studio, camera pointed at them. Pep band plays in the background.

> JOHN
> Good Morning America! Spring is right around the corner and I already smell love in the air.

> SUSAN
> That's right. We've had multiple successes and failures over the past few seasons, but I don't know, I think this may be the season for these youngsters to find their special someone.

> JOHN
> Oh, speaking of which, we have our first contestant coming in. We have JASON WILLIAMS, age 17, senior, class of 2018. His hobbies include bike riding and playing video games. He likes history and mathematics, and is head of the mathletes team.

> SUSAN
> Oh looky here, his target is no other than the senior beauty queen, TINA DAVIS. She's known for turning all the guys that come her way. We spoke with JASON last week and he's told us that he's, and I quote, "ready to take on the challenge and finally ask TINA out." Who

SUSAN (CONT'D)

knows…maybe JASON will be the lucky guy and kick off the season with a success. Right, JOHN?

JOHN

That's right. Speak of the devil, there's JASON.

SUSAN

Oh my. He looks so nervous. He's pacing back and forth in the hallway east of the 200 building.

EXT. THE PARK - DAY

JASON enters quickly and stiffly walking into the park.

JASON

Come on, JASON. You can do it. What's the worst that can happen. Remember, be cool.

SUSAN (V.O.)

I see her, she's a few yards down the hall. And here she comes. Oh boy, oh boy, now there's no going back.

Enter **TINA**. She is walking past JASON.

JASON

(clears his throat) H-hey TINA.

TINA

(stops to face JASON) Uh, Hi?

A small screen in the corner flickers on showing the sportscaster's reaction.

JOHN

(from the bottom of the screen) Uh-oh, what is this? Is she giving him attitude? This doesn't look good. It sounds like TINA doesn't want to see him.

SUSAN

Shh! Let's keep watching.

Small screen flickers off.

JASON

How are you?

                         TINA
Fine I guess.

                         JASON
Can I ask you something?

                       SUSAN (V.O.)
Oh my gosh, he's going for it.

                         TINA
Sure whatever.

                         JASON
So I was wondering, since the Valentine's Day dance is
coming up, would you want to go together?

                         TINA
What? You want me to go to the dance with you?

                       JOHN (V.O.)
Oh no, this is a mess. I'm anxious to see what happens.

                       SUSAN (V.O.)
So am I, but we'll see what happens when we return after
this brief commercial break.

ADVERTISEMENT

INT. BROADCASTING ROOM.

                         JOHN
Welcome back folks. We are here live with what looks like
a tragic proposal featuring JASON WILLIAMS and
TINA DAVIS. I'm your host, JOHN BROWN.

                         SUSAN
(sighs) And I'm SUSAN WALKER. I really hope this
doesn't turn out to be a failure. With past events JASON
had been seeming to do well during past sessions, but as
we mentioned, he still hasn't found the right girl. And it's
really heartbreaking to see that he might be let down
again.

                         JOHN
Let's take a look at some of the footage from earlier
today. Roll the clip.

EXT. PARK.

>JASON
>
>H-hey TINA.
>
>TINA
>
>Uh, Hi?

INT. BROADCASTING ROOM.

>JOHN
>
>There you see it. She doesn't look very happy to see him.

>SUSAN
>
>You're right, JOHN. But hey, it's been a long day. Maybe she's just in a bad mood. Perhaps it's better if he asks her tomorrow?

>JOHN
>
>Oh, I don't know. If he keeps waiting, his opportunity may slip away. But let's stop our silly talking and get back to the event.

EXT. PARK.

>TINA
>
>What? You want me to go to the dance with you?

>JASON
>
>Yeah. I've been meaning to ask you out for quite a while. So I think now will be the perfect time to get to know each other.

>TINA
>
>Listen, JASON, I'm flattered, but no. I can't go to the dance with you.

>SUSAN (V.O.)
>
>Oh no poor JASON.

>JOHN (V.O.)
>
>Tsk tsk tsk. How sad. The boy will be scarred for life.

                    JASON
Why not?

                    TINA
Well, you see, I'm already going with someone.

                    JASON
You are? Who?

                    TINA
AMANDA.

                SUSAN (V.O.)
What! Who is AMANDA?

                    TINA
AMANDA and I have been friends since we were
children and well I guess I've always seen her then more
than a friend. I guess the reason why I've never accepted
a guy was because I wasn't interested. I'm so sorry.

                 JOHN (V.O.)
Oh that's got to hurt.

                    JASON
It's okay. I'm just happy that you found someone that
you like. No hard feelings.

                                    SMASH CUT TO:

INT. BROADCASTING ROOM.

                JOHN and SUSAN
Aww.
                    SUSAN
He's such a sweet guy

                    JOHN
Yes he is. Any girl would be lucky to be with him.

                    SUSAN
Well folks that wraps up this week's broadcast. Stay
tuned to listen to an exclusive interview featuring

                     121

JASON WILLIAMS and TINA DAVIS. I'm your host
SUSAN WALKER.

                    JOHN
And I'm JOHN BROWN. See ya then.

[Screen shows a cheesy transition]

                    JOHN
Hello and welcome back to the show. We are your
hosts, JOHN BROWN.
                    SUSAN
And SUSAN WALKER. Let's take a recap of what
happened during the live event shall we. So during this
event we experienced a total plot twist. Senior, JASON
WILLIAMs, was looking forward to asking out fellow
classmate and beauty queen, TINA DAVIS, who is
known for her reputation for being difficult to approach
and has never agreed to date even the most popular and
gushed-over guys.

                    JOHN
That's right. So JASON had attempted to ask her to the
Valentine's Day dance and she did not accept, but that's
not the most shocking part of all. It turns out that she is
actually not interested in guys and has come to the
realization of having an interest in girls instead.

                    SUSAN
This is the first time we have ever experienced this
happening during the show and to talk about what
happened we have here in the studio with us, TINA
DAVIS and JASON WILLIAMS.

                    JOHN
Welcome to the show, guys.

                    TINA
Good afternoon thank you for having us.

                    JASON
It's a pleasure to be here.

SUSAN

It's our pleasure. So tell us JASON how were you feeling when you had found out that TINA was going to the dance with AMANDA?

JASON

I was of course upset that she had rejected me,but at the same time I felt a sense of relief for actually having the guts to tell her and that she accepted who she is and her ability to show bravery for who she likes.

JOHN

That's amazing. TINA, how did you feel to finally express yourself and your sexuality?

TINA

I feel like I have gotten a huge weight off of my shoulders. I knew there had to be a reason to always reject guys that have asked me out and now that I have finally found someone I like and feel comfortable around, I know the exact reason why.

SUSAN

You guys are amazing and we really need more students like you guys.

JOHN

So do you think this occasion will get you guys closer as friends?

JASON

Most definitely. We have actually decided to go to the dance as a group.

TINA

This way, we can finally get to know each other.

SUSAN

That's amazing. Thank you two for joining us here today.

JOHN

We hope you the best for the rest of the year and for your future after graduation.

JASON and TINA bow.

DIRECTOR (V.O.)

Cut!

FADE OUT.

BEACH DAY
By Monson Wilson

At the beach on hot sand
with the bright sun gazing down
On the ice cold ocean sparkling
And the sun in the sky darkening
As the wind grows chilly at night
The moon rises to fill the sky
Making the waves crash in the sand
Shaking the ground on the land
Watching the sunrise is beautiful
Best at the fall of night
With the clear blue sky
Watching the seagulls fly by and by
On a beautiful beach day.

UNDERSTAND
By Christine Do

I SLID MY HANDS across the counter. The cafe was having a rather busy Wednesday evening and, outside, patrons of the store stood freezing in the cold winter air. Thick puffs of air came from their mouths, a delicate mixture of hot and cold created a whirlwind of steam, much like those from the coffee cups. I stared up at the cat clock, its tail ticking to the beat. Five more minutes until my shift was over. I moved quicker, making three final cups of coffee. I looked over at my boss who simply waved me off with a quick shake of his head. I smiled, wiped the sweat off my forehead and ran to the backroom to change. While walking out, I got a text from my best friend, Rei: *Have fun babe and if he breaks your heart I'll be there to break his neck.*

I rolled my eyes, sighing. What could I possibly do without that girl?

I gave one final wave to my coworkers and headed out, squeezing through the crowd of people gathered near the door. I checked my phone again. He should have been here by—

The wind was knocked out of me as I was squashed into the arms of a large man.

"Erick, stop it," I said, giggling as I was let go.

He kissed me on the forehead. "Oh, stop, you love it."

My cheeks flushed. I took his hand and pulled him away from the cafe. I could see some of my coworkers making kissy faces through the window.

"How immature," Erick said.

I laughed, sticking my tongue out at them when he wasn't looking.

For the rest of the evening, Erick and I window-shopped along the snow-covered sidewalk, but I wasn't looking at anything other than him. I couldn't help but feel uncertain about him—about us.

It was that day I spent with Rei that got me thinking.

Rei and I had been walking to the campus cafeteria. It was mid-fall and winter was just around the corner. The leaves had begun to flutter down from the trees and were crushed underneath our feet as we walked.

"God, I have two projects due on the same week," I said. "I don't know if I can finish them."

Rei smacked me in the shoulder. "Shut up. You could finish them by tonight if you'd stop procrastinating by calling Erick all day."

"But…it's not that, but," I said.

"No buts. You know how important this to you. I'm sure he'll understand if you don't talk *all* the time."

I sighed. She was right. Boyfriend and girlfriend— it was just a title for now. We should focus on our lives and our futures above all. He had his engineering, and I had my fashion designing. Of course we would keep building good memories together.

I smiled fondly, glancing at Erick, intertwining our fingers together, and reminiscing how we first met.

It was at the cafe, back when he was still working there. He had already been on the job for two years and was showing me the ropes. I was a fast learner and quick with my hands considering the amount of time I spent drawing and doodling designs for my classes. Attending an art school was a tough job to keep up with, and the cafe was an add-on I should've avoided, but me being me, I couldn't help but want to make my own money. It wasn't that my parents weren't well endowed, but I felt that earning money on my own could teach me a good work ethic and help me make some new friends.

The people at the cafe were different: they were warm, like the atmosphere in the shop. Nothing felt awkward, especially not Erick. It was as if we knew each other from long ago, in a different time, a different past. It was like a dream getting to know him.

We had been working together for a year—took the guy long enough— before he asked out. But it was sweet that he waited to get to know me first. Our first date was amazing; it was a sunny day, quite the opposite from today. He had taken me to the beach where we held hands and bought junk food from nearly every pop-up shop available.

Unfortunately for us, our co-workers were also our closest friends. They were absolutely ridiculous, following us to the pier and trying to sneak around without us knowing. We were far from stupid, so we spent half the time playing around with their hearts. It may be cruel to put my arm around his neck with him holding me by the waist and pretending to lean in for a kiss, but it was all worth it to hear the groaning in the background. Eventually, we found peace in the Ferris wheel, kissing at the top where no one could see us. My heart nearly beat out of my chest at the feeling of being with him. My cheeks were hot as we got out of the cart, the conductor even winked at Erick who playfully winked back, earning a smack on the back from me. Our friends, who were on the cart behind us, ultimately got caught, and we spent the rest of the night playing the booth games all together.

I smiled up at Erick, who had nudged me. "Babe, you seem distracted. What is it?"

"Just remembering how we met, and our first date." I hummed. "Before you dropped your job at the cafe and got a real one at a large company."

"That was the best first date I've ever had in my entire life," he said, laughing. "The Ferris wheel, the games. My heart couldn't stop beating. Maybe it was all that playing around… or maybe it was the fact that I was with you."

Wow. He would never say something that cheesy. We always said stupid romantic things playfully, but the tone in his voice told me something else.

Erick stopped me there, the snow falling around us.

I looked up at him, getting lost in his hazel eyes. "Erick—"

"Do you recognize this place?"

I hesitated for a second, and then it came to me. "This is where we first had our second date. The old, lit-up bridge on 45th street, where you said—"

"—That my parents first got engaged."

He leaned toward me. I stopped him before he could get down on his knees and dragged him over to a bench beside the bridge.

He furrowed his eyebrows as he desperately searched into my eyes. My heart twisted in knots, but this needed to be done.

"I'm going to say this quick so that you don't feel hurt. I'm not rejecting you. I'm just going to simply tell you that we need to wait a bit." I took his hands in mine.

Erick blinked, his eyes wide.

"What? You know what I mean." I kissed him on the cheek. "C'mon, you're smart, you know neither of us have a stable job yet, right?"

It took him a minute but *eventually* he caught on. "But still—"

"Wait until I get a full time job first, then I'll consider it."

"But what am I supposed to tell the guys when I get back? I told them I was going to propose, and now I'm going to look lame." He pouted.

"Oh, please. Rei would shut them up before they could say a single thing."

"I guess you're right."

We sat in comfortable silence for a while. My head leaning on his shoulder and our hands intertwined.

Erick exhaled, letting out a puff of cold air. "You know, I should feel sad about this, but I don't."

"You are a crybaby." I had my hand over my mouth to keep from laughing.

He glared at me. "How dare you."

I mirrored his face teasingly. "And what are you going to do about it, hmm?"

"I'm going to marry you and you'll have to deal with this 'crybaby' for the rest of your life."

I stopped laughing. "How cruel of you."

We continued to shoot daggers for another second before we burst out laughing.

He threw a his arm around me, pulling me back to him.

"No, but seriously, you'll marry me, right?"

"Yes but—"

"Yeah, yeah, I know. Career first."

I grinned. "Now you're getting it."

THE SIMPLE THINGS
By Jackie Hermosillo

It's the simple things you do
The way you smile and laugh
When no one is around
The way you look at me
When I'm the one laughing.

Every day you make me smile
Even when I don't want to
You never let me stay angry
It's the way you make everything
work out exactly how it should

It's the way you pretend to be angry
When I don't return your hoodies
But the way you smile when I wear them
It says something more

It's the way you listen
Even when you don't want to
And the way you comfort me
through big things and small
It's the way you are

To others, you aren't perfect
But to me, you are the perfection I need
To me, being you is what makes you perfect
It's just the simple things

TOY
By Vy Le

You tell me not to fall in love with you
Because you don't deserve such a thing like that
Oh, how nice and sweet you are
And I am wrong about you.
You tell me not to get close to you
But you are the one who comes closer to me
You are the one who says, "I love you."
You tell me not to care about you
But when I force myself not to
You are the one who asks me why.
Maybe I'm just your toy
You pull my strings like a puppet
Giving me false hope,
Flirting with me only when you're bored,
Asking me to love you when you want to be loved,
But never loving me back.
I am drawn to you
Even though it hurts,
I still want to love you.

DIMENSIONS OF THE SOUL

By Aithy Nguyen

Intricate strings crossing over one another
Devils and angels clashing
A hand in fragrant oils
Fall into the cold endless waters
Watch as the blinding sun shrinks from above
The body swallowed whole by an invisible beast
A babe is born
A rose petal falls
Walk the earth into the dry deserts
Walk the earth into the valley of thorns
Lay on the soft bed
Stare at the twinkling stars
See in me
For I am the soul
And these are my dimensions

THE FINAL BATTLE
By Phuong Traceyle

THE MIGHTY CHEETAH RELAXES under the shade of a tree on the savannah. He lies there, purring softly, relieved to be out of the scorching sun. Dark spots on his skin stretch over his thin, muscular body.

By the huge rock near the lake a powerful hawk perches, waiting for his food to come by. His brown feathers and black tipped wings make him easily recognizable. In the distance, the slight movements of a gazelle catches the attention of the two predators. The cheetah and hawk stare at it hungrily, approaching the unknowing gazelle side-by-side.

"I will get this gazelle," the hawk whispers to himself.

The cheetah snaps, "Don't you dare, you ugly bird. It's mine."

"Who are you calling an ugly bird? Fight me," the hawk responds.

The cheetah stretches his limbs, preparing for the attack. The hawk watches tentatively and spreads his wings. The cheetah looks up, glaring. "What is he doing?"

The hawk swoops down and taps the cheetah, making him jolt with surprise.

"I know. You want to play tag? I'll catch you." The cheetah pounces on the hawk with his sharp claws. The hawk clings onto the cheetah using his huge talons.

"Let me go!" The hawk shouts.

"No, you let go!" The cheetah yells.

They release each other, blood dripping from their bodies. Startled by the fight, the gazelle moves to safety.

"You patchy kitty-cat," the hawk yells, "you scared the gazelle away."

The cheetah glares at him. "You started it first."

The wounded animals return home without a meal.

The next day, worn from their injuries, the cheetah and hawk rest in the shade. They look at each other with tired eyes and turn to see who's by the field. Instead of a calm gazelle, an antelope is enjoying a grassy snack. The cheetah stares at it with a watering mouth.

The hawk looks at the antelope, then the cheetah. "While that kitty looks at the antelope, this is my chance to get it." He takes to the air.

The cheetah, desperate for a meal, sprints towards the antelope. The antelope hears a rumble and gallops away. The two predators take chase. This antelope is one quick rascal. As the cheetah pounces on it, the hawk grabs onto the antelope's neck and pulls away.

The cheetah growls. "Hey! I caught it first. Give it back."

The cheetah and hawk turn on each other, leaving the antelope, with a wounded neck, to limp away from them. The hawk smacks the cheetah with its wing and flies off. The cheetah looks down with disappointment and cries over his lost meal.

After those two days of intense battles, the cheetah and hawk visit the watering hole for a cool drink. They glanced at each other while drinking. They remember that moment, the two bloody battles between them just for one meal. Their entire bodies are sore from beating and wrestling each other. They rest by the tree for shade, hawk among the leaves and the cheetah on the ground.

A hare hops from the bushes.

"That baldy bird will steal the food even if I claim it," the cheetah says.

"I am hungry just by thinking about the battle," the hawk says.

The hare hops from one brush to another.

"I can't resist staring at that rabbit," the cheetah says and starts sprinting towards the hare.

"No! Why, I will end this battle once and for all," the hawk responds and flies towards the cheetah.

The two predators fight for the last time. The final battle starts now. The hare looks up and upon seeing the two hungry animals, hops away to its burrow. As the cheetah sprints with high speed, the hawk swoops down and grabs the cheetah by the tail, pulling the cheetah to slow down.

"Hey you bird, let go of my tail!" the cheetah shouts.

"I won't let go unless I get my food," the hawk says and tries to pull the cheetah farther away from the hare's burrow.

The cheetah turns around and pounces on the hawk with hiss mighty paws.

"Stop!" he hawk shouts.

The cheetah stops and lets go. "What now?" the cheetah asks.

"We never catch our meals because we always fight each other. We need to find an easier way to get food," the hawk says.

"Maybe we can work together? That way, we can both catch food to eat without getting injured from the battle," the cheetah says.

"I guess we can try," the hawk agrees.

The hare still eats the grass.

"Are you ready?" the cheetah asks with anticipation.

"Ready," the hawk answers.

The cheetah sprints toward the hare, while the hawk flies above it. The hawk swoops down and grab the hare's head, while the cheetah pounces on the hare's back.

"We did it!" the cheetah says.

The cheetah and hawk go back to their places and eat their wild-caught meal. The final battle is a success.

WATERCOLOR
By Vylan Tran

My feelings are all mixed up.
I don't know how I feel.
The darkness inside of me.
Mixed with the light that comes throughout the day.
The sadness that seeks within, pours out.
Feeling the pain.
My eyes release the tears.
For a moment.
The sun gleams through my face.
My lips.
They move to the sun.
My eyes shine bright as the sun.
joy overcomes everything.
But, one little thing.
Can ruin that moment.
That one dot of black.
Changes everything.

THE WORLD HE WALKS

By Jackie Hermosillo

He walks along the earth
listening to all and everything
Yet, to nothing at all
Too engulfed in his own sorrow
One that he hides from all

To others he seems fine, he seems *okay*
When the reality is
he's drowning within himself,
in *his* own inescapable prison
That was made just for him

He tried to be okay, he really did
but he just couldn't
His pain was a mystery to even him
"How could I possibly feel like this?
What am I feeling?"
He never got an actual answer

It's funny how quickly time changes
how different it can be interpreted
To some, time is short and fleeting
While other see it as a lasting cycle
To him, he can't decide which is best

But he continues to walk
Trying to figure out his emotions,
Navigating through the paths they take him
But he still goes on, continues through
The world he walks

GOPHERS

By Johnson Nguyen

There are many types of gophers
big or small
skinny or fat
But I love them all
They live in holes
They like being alone
Gophers don't like packs
They live by themselves.
I don't know why
If I did, I'd be lonely
Then I would cry.
But they still talk to each other
By making huge tunnels
So they can collect food
It looks like a puzzle.
Gophers live in many places—
North and Central America
They live among the vast plains
Or even cooler yet—
along the coastal areas.

MY BEST FRIEND

By HongAnh Nguyen

I hold you dearly,
Close to my heart.
You are a ray of sunshine,
That brightens the dark.

You're genuinely kind,
Hopeful, and happy.
You're a leaning shoulder of support,
Whenever I'm gloomy.

Everything about you,
Is so precious to me,
From the freckles on your nose,
To your sweet personality.

The way that you write,
To the way that you laugh,
Is original and cute,
And I love it deeply.

Words can't describe
How valuable I hold you to be,
My dorky best friend,
Who's taller than me.

MORNING WITH ZACH
By Vy Ngo

Characters:
Tom - sportscaster
Benedict - sportscaster
Cameraman - cameraman
Zach - young man; the unknowing star of a TV show

Setting:
England, Sandwich Sports Channel
Time:
Morning

Stage is split in half. A TV studio is on stage left. A kitchen, separated by a wall is on stage right. There are bushes on the edge of stage right, just outside of the kitchen window. In the kitchen there is a table alongside the wall with a phone, opposite the window. There is a stove/ oven and counter along the front, so audience can see someone cooking. Lights are on stage left only. Stage right is dark.

Show enters with a sight of the two Englishmen enjoying a brief talk on stage left. They are sitting behind a counter in a TV studio. The camera is placed in front of them and they turn to the camera with a smile.

Tom: Hello, Benedict. What a nice morning, ain't it?

Benedict: Why, yes, Tom, thank you. Welcome everyone to the Sandwich Sports channel. Today, we will be observing Zachary Mondane and his morning routine. Keep in mind that he does not know we're filming him, so he'll be much pleased once he finds out there's an entire audience just eagerly awaiting his arrival.

139

Tom: We have a cameraman right outside Zach's window, let's try not to get caught, eh. Ladies and gentlemen, "Morning with Zach!"

[*Relaxing jazz music starts to play and lights go on, illuminating the kitchen on stage right. Zach is in the kitchen on stage right, preparing breakfast.*]

Benedict (stage left): Look what we have here. Zach has just woken up from a long night's sleep. Robes, bags under eyes, bed head, and a grouchy expression. The typical morning Englishman.

Tom : Zach reaches for the coffee grinder. Oh, the sound of freshly ground coffee is just wonderful. What is this? Zach just scored two eggs into a porcelain bowl where he strikes them with a fork.

Benedict: Looks like those deadlifts paid off after all. I mean, look at the speed at which he's beating them. Those suckers got nothin' on my boy Zach.

[*Zach is preparing coffee with a coffee maker on the counter. There is a frying pan on the stove*]

Tom: Yeah, attack that coffee!

Benedict: The way he's pouring the water is definitely complex. Fantastic!

Tom: He's grabbing for that bacon. He's grabbing for that bacon. [*Zach is placing bacon into the frying pan.*] Grease that pan, Zach. [*Zach pours oil into oil into the frying pan.*] Don't let the bacon defeat you.

Benedict: Ladies and gentlemen, will Zach grease the pan? We'll find out right here at "Morning with Zach" after a quick commercial break.

[All on on stage freeze. Lights dim while we hear radio ads. *"Beware when you go outside," "The government is always watching"* and *"orange juice"* commercials plays. Lights brighten afterward.]

Benedict: And we're back with "Morning with Zach"

Tom: Zach just put bacon in the nicely greased pan. Oh! Look at those feisty bacon strips as they pop-chicka-pop with the oil. But listen to the sizzling. [He imitates the sizzling sound.]

Zach: *[turns toward the window and bushes because he hears some rustling in the bushes]* What was that? Probably a bunny.

Tom: Phew, that was a close one. Be careful, cameraman!

[*Cameraman inches on stage, crouching down behind bushes. He is holding a camera with an attached mic, both pointed in Zach's direction.*]

Benedict: The coffee looks about done. Zoom in on that wonderful coffee.

[*Cameraman inches upstage from his hiding place to get a good view of the coffee but trips*]

Zach: Hey, who's there? Why are you outside my window?

Cameraman: *[breathes heavily, panting as he takes cover again behind the bushes]*

Zach: *[picks up the receiver of a corded phone to call the cops. He forgets about the bacon. Operator is voice offstage.]*

Operator: *[from offstage]* 999 what's your—

Zach: Help! Some guy is outside my window with a camera, filming me.

Operator: What's your name and address?

Zach: My address is 7890 Moug Ave, Northminster.

Operator: Okay, and, again, what is your name?

Zach: Zachary Mondane. Come quickly.

[Stagehand behind the stove/oven outside of audience view, obviously raises up a hand, holding what looks like a fire over the frying pan. This implies the bacon burns and sets the pan on fire. Zach trips on the phone wire as he tries to put out the fire. The fire alarm screams. The cameraman runs away.]

Zach: (panicked and jumping up and down) Holy shizzle sticks! My bacon's on fire! I tried to chase him out b-but my kitchen caught on fire after I reached for the phone.

Operator: [sigh] Okay. What do you need? An ambulance, a firetruck...?

Zach: You're the operator, you're supposed to know!

Operator: Alright, alright. I'll send a team to you. Just wait for a few minutes.

Zach: (drops the phone and runs in circles) What's going on...?

Benedict: [*stutters*] Well, that's all for now. Tune in next time for a brand new episode.

Tom: See ya!

Zach: (Stands in place) Is that why they gave me $5 to sign that paper? I should've read the terms and conditions.

[Relaxing outro music plays as Zach is left very confused and afraid]

EPHEMERAL SUMMER DAYS
By Thanh Le

How I long for old days of a marvelous blue
Where I sat on the lake's edge with nothing to do
But gaze upon the water and its thread-like waves
Made by the winds of summer's day

My hand dances on the surface like the insects
Who tread ever so carefully, as they fear death
Dragonflies hover, seeking prey to intercept
They swoop, before one can take breath

I pick up a rock and throw it with all my might
It skips twice before it falls, leaving a great splash
How I wish I could skip rocks late into the night
Though, clumsy me, would slip and crash.

Frogs croak on lily pads, birds chirp in the distance
Such lovely images, in my reminiscence
With every passing year, memories grow duller
May I return one day to the lake, of a lovely blue color.

FINAL FRONTIER
By Edison Sesmas

Reposing by the hearth's gaping mouth,
The blood-red cinder expelling
Fiery sparks that dance on the cabin's dark floor,
My thoughts revert to the past.

I have had it all.
had friends, bountiful and faithful.
I have done it all, traveled from the Earth's
Ends and into unknown depths.

Yet the final frontier awaits:
The unknown that has puzzled man for
Centuries—I will be one of many to
Experience the passing between life and death.

Dozing off into nothingness,
I fall into a deep slumber.

THE STAR
By Kelly Ho

I fell in love with a star
One that shines brighter than the sun
The one that burns with passion
The one that keeps shining until it's done

I fell in love with the stars
The ones that live in his eyes
They shine bright in the night
And never seem to die

I fell for his smile on the ground
The way he asked, "Will you be mine?"
I fell for everything he said
Even if they were lies

I fell too hard into love
And I still jump back in
I know it'll hurt more
but my heart always returns

Though you hurt me with those lies
Though I know you aren't mine
I continue to love you with all of me
Leaving my cares behind

You are too far for me to reach
But I'm glad you're happy there
You're a star and I am not
This fact I'm well aware.

DISTANCE
By Krista Phanpraphou

We are different, though we talk
We're so far, yet we're friends
Across the globe,
You and I
Think, write, and press send
We don't know much about each other,
But we're close
No one knows about you
No one knows about me
I'm your secret
And you are mine
I will soon graduate,
And so will you
talking is difficult
Communication is key
But how can that be?
We live in different places
And that's hard for us
You're in the cold
I'm in the heat
You see snow
I see sun
I'm from the great land of liberty
You're from a great land, 'Thou, Ancient, Thou Free'
My emotions are bundled,
In a tight bottle
I wonder if we are indeed possible
Feelings change, and you know it too
I question your loyalty
I question you
Will it be the same when we see each other?
Will it be the same after we graduate?

As each day passes,
We grow older
Feelings fade away, and I fear losing
My only gift to you is our times spent together
I may not be the one
But I can be a great friend
We may never see each other
But I hope we meet at least once
What I wish for you
Is your happiness and our remaining months

GRATITUDE
By Krista Phanpraphou

We share a connection,
And I am grateful

When you're awake,
I am asleep.
And during your sleep,
I am awake.
We try to connect,
And keep it together
Even though you are tired,
You stay up with me
Listening to my rants,
accepting my stupidity.
We call during weekends,
And I am happy.
Like others, we talk
But I'll never forget your comfort
I feel like a child,
Being patted on the head
Listening to your words of reassurance
As I dig into your chest.
On the other side of the screen,
My heart is filled with joy.
On the other side of the screen,
I imagine you smiling.
I wish to be friends along the run,
And give you my appreciation
Because I am grateful,
For you being the one.

CONTINUE THE STORY
By Aithy Nguyen

THEON WAS DETERMINED TO find the legendary miracle waters—waters that granted immunity from all suffering and the promise of eternal life.

As the stories went, a woman named Seraphine discovered the fountain of youth. She had been plagued by leprosy, an illness that could not be cured by any medicine or remedy.

Exiled by her village, she had nothing, knew nothing, and was nothing. Coming to the conclusion that she should end her own life swiftly before the disease did, she planned to drown herself in a pond she had stumbled upon. However, death was not the result. As she rose out of the cooling waters, she found that she was no longer marked with spots.

Returning to her village in hopes that her people would welcome her home, she was stunned to find that they had instead condemned her for sorcery. She pleaded to them many times, claiming that she was healed by sacred waters; however, her words were ignored, so she fled, never to be seen again.

Many generations passed, and Seraphine's tale transformed into myth.

Theon would find that pond. He finished writing his departing letter to his parents and thus began his search for the fountain of youth. He set off on his journey.

A voice downstairs interrupted Wyatt's writing.

"Wyatt!" his father yelled. "Get down here this instant. Our guests are here."

"Yes, Dad." Wyatt quickly retreated from his typewriter. He changed into a pair of decent trousers and a clean button up. He ran a hand through his curly brown hair, undoing the knots as he descended the stairs. When his father spotted him, Wyatt stiffened. He hated whenever his father brought guests over to the house; Wyatt was always expected to be present, but he never understood why. Even so, he sat down at the table with his father and his guests.

"Henry," Nicholas said, "this is my son, Wyatt."

Wyatt nodded.

The man called Henry was short and chubby, well into his fifties. A girl about Wyatt's age sat beside him.

"Wyatt," Nicholas said, pointing across the table, "this is my new partner, Henry Campbell, and his lovely daughter, Violet Campbell."

Wyatt responded with the script he used whenever his father would introduce him to a new business partner. "A pleasure, Mr. Campbell. As you, Ms. Campbell." He smiled as if he genuinely enjoyed their company. "What brings you here today, might I ask?"

Henry chuckled and turned to Wyatt's father. "A polite boy you have here, Nicholas." He looked back at Wyatt. "There will be much talk in the future, young man, but today is simply a day for introductions."

"You will be staying for dinner, I presume?" Nicholas asked.

Wyatt cleared his throat. The last time his father invited a guest to dinner, he was expected to sit through hours of talk he never cared for.

"Of course," Henry said. "How could I refuse?"

Violet surveyed the house without paying much attention to the conversation.

"Violet," said Henry, nudging her and looking at Nicholas. "I'm sorry. Violet here tends to have a very short attention span. The girl has a vivid imagination."

Wyatt's father grinned. "It's quite alright." He focused his attention on Violet. "Violet, your father has told me you have a talent for painting. Is that right?"

She beamed and sat up straighter. "I don't like to brag, but I do love art."

Nicholas nudged his son's leg under the table.

Wyatt cringed then returned to wearing his best pleasant expression.

"Detailed and mysterious as the works of Leonardo da Vinci," Nicholas asked, "or as abstract as the works of Pablo Picasso?"

Violet smirked at Wyatt for a split second, right before returning to her composed state.

"Van Gogh," she said.

Nicholas nudged Wyatt with his elbow. "Son, isn't that lovely?"

"Van Gogh wasn't one of the options," Wyatt said.

Violet smoothed the creases in her dress. "I didn't like the options I was given." She smirked again, but somehow neither Nicholas nor Henry noticed.

Wyatt noticed. "And who said you could change the options because they didn't meet your criteria?" He paused. "Violet is it? The question of your preference between the two aforementioned artists was simple enough—"

"Wyatt." His father looked at him sternly.

What came after was one of the longest uncomfortable silences that Wyatt ever experienced.

"Wyatt won't be joining us for dinner," his father finally said.

Wyatt stood and excused himself from the table, exchanging another round of pleasantries before ascending the stairs. He knew he would hear from his father later. In the meantime, his typewriter beckoned him.

Three days had never felt like such an eternity to Theon. He was sore and too exhausted to continue any further in the strange forest, so he made camp beside a river bank. He spread out his blanket and lay on it, the rocky surface underneath pricking at his back. He gazed at the stars in the night sky to pass the time. It was not long until he found himself swallowed by the dark.

Wyatt was startled by a knock at his door.

"It's open." He expected his father to come and scold him for his behavior, but was instead greeted by Violet.

"Your room is so…" She tapped her chin. "Dull."

Wyatt mumbled some scathing insults.

"What did you say?" she asked.

He found that forged smile of his. "Nothing."

She shrugged, and made her way over to him. "What are you typing?"

He got up instantly and stood between her and the typewriter. "Nothing."

She crossed her arms. "Now I really want to know what you are hiding."

"If you think I'll be a gentleman and show you, you're less intelligent than I assumed." He scoffed. "Forget it. Now leave my room."

Violet narrowed her eyes, but then gave him a large grin. "What if, let's say, hypothetically, I were to march downstairs and interrupt your father's dinner?" She laughed. "How about I say you spat in my face?" She gasped. "Or worse, that you threatened to murder my entire family and me if I

151

didn't leave your room?" She slowly paced back and forth in front of him. "Is that any way to treat a guest?"

He couldn't remember the last time he had felt such hatred for someone. He clenched his fists. "You wouldn't."

She pursed her lips. "Oh? You think I care what your father will do to you? You think I have sympathy for a boy I've only just met a few hours ago? Much less one that was so impolite to me?"

His façade broke. "You don't. Nor would I for a stranger. But don't," he said. "Two weeks ago my father locked me in here with no food for two days for simply forgetting to water the garden. Don't do this to me."

She turned her gaze to the wooden floors of his room, then back at him. "Then tell me. What are you writing?"

Theon kept his eyes shut but knew he wasn't alone.
The unknown figure moved closer.
A boar perhaps? Or could it be a jaguar? Running wouldn't be the best idea— the animal would give chase. Regardless, Theon was ready to pounce when it was close enough. He heard the sound of a twig snapping, and then rummaging.
The creature was going through what few food rations Theon had, and he could not afford to lose any more. At the last second, he quickly shot up from his blanket and tackled the animal.

"What type of animal is it?" Violet asked.

Wyatt shrugged. "Why do you annoy me with so many pointless questions?"

"You don't know?"

"You can't just force ideas to come, Violet."

"You ought to become a lawyer or a businessman like your father. Why a writer? From the looks of it, you aren't that good of one anyway."

"One, I don't want to be anything like my father," he said. "Two, if I wasn't a good writer, you wouldn't be here discussing it with me."

She laughed. "That may be true, but your story needs flavor."

"Flavor?" he asked. "That's absurd. It's not like I can add salt to it."

"Metaphorically speaking, you need something that isn't bland. Something to give the story a little kick. Salt."

"Salt." He thought for a bit. "Ridiculous." Before he could say anything further, his father burst into the room.

"Wyatt!" he exclaimed. "Good news."

"What is it, Father? Has something happened?"

"This was just delivered." Nicholas waved a letter in his hand. "It is for you, son."

Wyatt took the letter from his father.

"Remember when you enlisted?" his father said. "You'll finally be a man now, won't you, son?" Nicholas said. He left the room before Wyatt could ask what he meant.

Wyatt opened the letter and his eyes widened. He could hear his father chatting about it with Henry downstairs.

"What is it, Wyatt?" Violet asked, trying to look over his shoulder to see the letter. "What does it say?"

He gulped. "The army. I'm going to fight in the army."

Seven months passed since the enlistment letter had arrived. Wyatt had thought the first day he saw Violet would be the last time he would ever hear from her. He was sorely disappointed as she was persistent in sending him letters every day. Strange, as he thought she hated him as much as he hated her.

His father demanded he reply to her to be kind, so he had no other choice but to do so. There wasn't much to say at first, but they found some common ground in their attempt to continue his story. It didn't progress much; they had found little time for it while he was going through basic military training. Regardless, she would manage to find an opportunity to talk in those letters, especially about art.

Despite not seeing each other, Wyatt had been grateful to her for having a change of heart towards him. For once, his writing wasn't his only companion. For those seven months, Wyatt would write letters to a young woman for whom his resentment was receding, finding himself falling for her with each passing day. He still remembered her black, wavy hair and indigo eyes as if it was yesterday.

Finally, the day came for his deployment overseas. There was news of a second World War breaking out in Europe.

Wyatt stood by his father waiting at the train station. Many others were saying goodbye to their families and friends.

"I hate to say it, Wyatt, but it does not appear that she's coming," Nicholas said. "Perhaps Violet did not have the heart to see you head out."

Wyatt looked away and huffed. He began to think that for once his father was right until he spotted a girl with wavy black locks making her way to them.

Violet reached them, panting. "Sorry. I'm not very good with directions, you see. Am I late?"

Wyatt grinned. "Yes, yes you are."

"I'll give you both a moment alone." Nicholas walked back into the crowd.

Violet finally caught her breath. "You look… dashing."

He put his hands in his pockets. "And you look the same."

She twirled her hair. "That is because I was afraid you wouldn't recognize me if I did anything else."

He rolled his eyes. "Of course. You are such a considerate soul."

She let out a breath. "So…" she started. "You're leaving."

He nodded. "Quite obvious, is it not?"

She smiled. "Yes, but I didn't think you would go through with it."

"For the first time, my father doesn't see me as a nuisance, and I was the one who wanted this. Now that I think of it, I'm not sure why I enlisted. But it's too late to have second thoughts now, isn't it?"

She paused. "Will you still write to me?"

His hands came out of his pockets and he put them on her shoulders. "Only if you stop talking about those damned paintings all the time."

She chuckled. "Yes. But promise me that you'll keep writing that story of yours."

He raised a brow. "I thought you once said I wasn't that good of a writer."

Her face brightened. "You know what I meant. Send me a new part every time you write. I've wanted to know how much salt you can add."

He hesitated then nodded as the train came into the station. "The train is here. I'd best get going."

His father returned to hug him goodbye.

"Good luck, son. Make me proud." Nicholas patted his son on the back. "Off you go."

As Wyatt boarded the train, he could not help but look back at the lovely girl he was leaving behind.

Theon quickly retreated from the figure he thought was an animal. "Elide?! What the hell are you doing here?"

She stood, brushing the dirt off her clothes. "I could ask the same of you, Theon. What are you doing, traveling for more than three days in the middle of the forest?"

He couldn't decide if he should tell her. "Go home, Elide."

She did not move. "I've been following you for days. At least tell me what you're up to."

The sun had just risen. He had to find the fountain soon before his food ran out. Best to get her out of the way. "I'm searching for the fountain of youth," he simply said. "Good enough? You can go now." He pushed past her, but she wouldn't have it.

"I'm coming with you." She latched onto his arm.

He had not expected that answer. The statement of the fountain of youth should have convinced her that he was on a fool's errand. "You can't come," he said.

"And why not?"

"The forest is dangerous. Go home."

"So it's safer to just leave me to go back alone?" Elide tightened her grip. "We grew up together. Your family was my family. You were even once betrothed to me for goodness sake. You know I can't just leave you here."

He was silent.

"Don't be like this," she said. "Just because you married someone else, doesn't mean I can't keep caring for you."

He went red. "You know I didn't do it because I loved her. You know that. I had no other choice."

She shook her head. "That doesn't matter anymore. She's your wife now. We can't change the past. But if you think I'm leaving, then you don't know me as well as I thought you did."

He swallowed. "So what do you propose? To come with me to find a mythical pond?" he asked.

"Precisely," she said. "Come on, then. The day isn't going by any slower."

⋆   ⋆   ⋆

Wyatt could not take back what he saw, or rather, what he had lived through. The sound of gunshots, the sight of bloodied bodies carpeting the ground, the impact of bombs obliterating towns. He had killed his first enemy and watched as the life escaped the soldier's eyes. The only thing keeping him sane was the letter that arrived from home.

Dearest Wyatt,

It seems you are an expert when it comes to adding flavor, transitioning from a simple child's tale to a heartstopping story of love, magic, and adventure. Genius. I believe your new approach is much more promising than that animal you were going to incorporate. What were you going to do with it anyway? Make Theon kill the beast, and then eat it?

Nothing much has changed at home. My father continues to meet with your father regularly, and I am left alone to contemplate. It is hard for me to admit, but I do find it rather boring here with you gone. I have come to miss our pointless arguments. We did not see each other often before, or ever much at all for that matter, but I do feel a sense of longing for you. I miss you dearly and count the days until your return. I know you don't find a liking for art, but I believe I can change that. Just you wait and see Wyatt Hayes. No man has ever escaped my charms. You may not be the brightest of the lot, Wyatt, but it just so happens that I'm quite fond of you. Till the time comes, I'll be waiting for your next letter.

With love,

Violet Campbell

Violet rushed to the door and opened it as the mailman arrived.

"Frank, anything for me today?" she asked.

"Yes ma'am," he said. "And a couple for your father as well."

She grabbed the small stack and went back to her unfinished biscuit, tearing the envelope addressed to her open without caring about the mess she made.

February 1, 1943

My Dear Violet,

I must tell you how peculiar you are. When I first met you, you would enrage me so much so that I thought my head would explode. But these days, I am more than thrilled to hear from you. In any case, I am glad to be writing you this letter. This war will soon be at an end, hopefully, so don't worry. I'll be home before you know it. It is true I do not care much for paintings, and do very much think no one, not even a pretty girl such as yourself, can change that. Though, I am eager to find out what you have in store for me.

Can the famous Violet Campbell make a fan of Van Gogh out of me? We shall see. Until then, I have kept my word and have written the next part of my story.

> *Sincerely,*
> *Wyatt Hayes*

Wyatt wrapped his blanket tighter around him. Because of the cold, he could see his breath with each exhale. He had been wounded in the leg, but not so much that he was bedridden. As the wind blew across the camp, he picked up his pen, and began to write.

December 13, 1943

My Dear Violet,

I have visited the infirmary three times already. Nothing to fret about, just keeping you informed. The war gets bloodier by the day, and the men can't last much longer. You couldn't imagine how broken they are. Sometimes I don't even know if they're alive or not. I know about a month ago I said I would have written another part of the story. Sadly, I have not been able to do so, however, it is slowly coming together.

> *Till we meet again,*
> *Wyatt Hayes*

After he sent the letter, he lay silently in his tent, looking at a small picture of a deep black haired girl he held in his hand.

There was a sound. It grew louder. Theon held her tightly. "Don't be afraid," he said. Elide was rigid against him. "I'm not."

He was firm in tone. "Listen to me, whatever you do, do not move."

"Why?" she asked. "What if whatever's out there kills us?"

He repeated. "Do not move, even the slightest of motion will cause the water to swallow you whole."

"Water? What water—"

She was cut off by the flowing water beneath her feet. Slowly, the water rose. Above her ankles, then above her knees. Fear shone in her eyes as she held Theon in a solid hold. She fought the urge to shiver as the icy waters made it up her waist. "How is this possible?" she whispered.

He did not answer. She took her final gulp of air as the water overlapped her head, and she was submerged into the depths of the blue sea.

Wyatt's leg begun to tingle. He tapped it a couple times and continued writing.

> *She could not breath, and no matter how much she wanted to move, she refrained. If this is what death felt like, then she wouldn't have it any other way, than to die next to the man she loved. As the last of her willpower began to fade, the water descended, leaving both her and Theon dry. She opened her eyes to see the two of them standing amidst a luxurious garden in front of a spring of water. "It can't be," she said.*
>
> *Theon nodded. "The fountain of youth."*
>
> *As he made his way towards it, Elide cried out. "Wait. What are you doing?"*
>
> *He turned back at her. "I am going to bathe in it, and be granted the gift of youth."*
>
> *"You can't be serious," she said. "What if it's only an ordinary pond? Think about this thoroughly, will you?"*
>
> *Before he could utter a word, the pool gurgled. It looked like a pot of boiling broth, only no steam rose from the bubbles.*
>
> *They both witnessed a stunning young woman emerge from the water and reveal herself to them. She was unlike anyone Elide had ever seen.*
>
> *"You have journeyed far, I presume," the woman said. "My compliments. You have found the fountain of youth."*
>
> *They both stayed mute.*
>
> *The feminine figure made her way out of the water. "My name is Seraphine, and I am the keeper of the fountain."*
>
> *Elide finally spoke. "It exists. The fountain of youth exists."*

A loud knock on her front door startled Violet. Violet opened it, revealing an older uniformed man she had never before seen.

"I am looking for a Violet Campbell," he said.

"I'm Violet," she said. "What is it you are here for, sir?"

He took off his black hat. "May I come in for a bit?"

She bit her lip. "I am not really supposed to let strangers in, sir. Maybe if you would come back when my father—"

"It's concerning Mr. Wyatt Hayes," he said.

She let him in.

Wyatt's vision was beginning to fail. He could barely see the nurse as she approached.

"How much pain are you in?" the nurse asked.

He coughed and vomited into the bucket next to him. "I can manage," he said.

"What is your name, soldier?"

"Hayes. Wyatt Hayes."

"Mr. Hayes," the nurse said. "I'm afraid the infection has spread from your leg to the rest of your body. You won't be able to survive. The only thing you can do at this point is pray. The pain will only get worse from here."

His breathing became shallow, and the sweat dripping from his head dampened the pillow. "How long?"

"Two days, at most," she said. "There's nothing else we can do for you. I'm sorry."

He pointed to his jacket hung up and told her to get a picture out of the right pocket. The nurse rummaged through the pocket and took out a photo of a fair young lady with black wavy hair, and as she turned around, she found Mr. Hayes smiling, staring into nothingness.

She held her chest where her heart pounded and sobbed.

"My condolences, Ms. Campbell. He was a good soldier. He fought very bravely."

She almost choked on her tears. "Why him?" She wept harder. "He said he was coming home."

The old man gave her a bag. "These were his things. Most of them were meant for you." He left her to cry alone.

She calmed herself before looking through his items. She reached in the bag to find a letter addressed to her. Her hands shook as she opened it.

December 19, 1943

Violet, My Darling,

Should this letter find you well, it means I never made it back to you. Knowing you, at this moment you are probably crying your eyes out, and as I probably can assume, I never got to finish that story for you. As I was writing it, I can tell you that I felt much more connected to Theon than I ever would have thought possible. I thank you for that, for you, after all, were the one who pushed me to follow this passion of mine.

Knowing this war would have been the end of me, I chose to give you up altogether, and I am sorry for that. I am sorry that I was too afraid to tell you the truth of my

159

injury, and that I was dying. Forgive me. And I am sorry I could not give you the life you deserved. Don't cry too much over me, I am hardly worth it.

Tell my father he needn't bother showing up at my funeral. I'd prefer it if he wasn't there.

Again, before I disappear from your life forever, thank you for everything. You have been one of the greatest blessings of my life, and I am going to miss your wonderful curls and your endless talks of how great of a painter Van Gogh was.

Love,

Wyatt Hayes

As she continued to look through his belongings, Violet suddenly burst into tears once more as she held in her palm a beautiful gleaming wedding ring.

"How long have you been alive?" Theon asked.

"Over a century," Seraphine said. "After my people cast me out, I took refuge here and became the guardian of the fountain."

"On whose accord?" Elide asked.

"My own," Seraphine said. "Where else would I have gone? The fountain's waters saved my life, so I owe it my own as service."

Theon's breath grew faster by the second.

Seraphine examined him. "And why, pray tell, do you seek eternal youth?" she asked.

Theon looked to Elide. "Because I don't want to live my short life the way it is. I don't want to spend my life with a woman I don't love and watch as the one I do love never becomes mine."

Seraphine blinked. "And so you want to be immortal to outlive your suffering and then finally be with the one you desire," she said. "But what happens when she, a mortal one, grows old and deteriorates into dust? Who will you love then?"

He never removed his sight from Elide. "If she takes from the fountain and becomes youthful as I, we can live the rest of our lives only with each other."

Elide thought she had heard it wrong, but Theon's serious gaze said otherwise. She took a step back. "No, I will not do it."

He narrowed his eyes. "Elide, don't you see? If we both take it, we can start anew. We can be happy again. Isn't that what you want?"

Elide shook her head. "Theon, I love you more than anyone on this Earth, but don't ask me to do the unthinkable. I would rather perish than live the life you are offering me now. I want to grow old, I want to have children, I want to live my life no matter how short it is. That is how life is, Theon. How it was made to be and given to us. What you want is based purely out of greed."

160

There was a long silence while Theon stared at her.

Seraphine finally spoke again. "Well, what is your decision then?"

Theon fell to his knees. "Elide," he said. "You can never be with me then."

Elide shook her head. "You are wrong. I will always be there, no matter where. You will never lose me. You have a wife. Take responsibility for that choice. We may not always be together, but I will always cherish you. I will always love you for who you are." She walked over and knelt beside him. "I can't force you to do what you don't want, so this is entirely up to you. But I do ask that you leave it behind." She reached for his hand. "This isn't the right way to live, Theon. What will happen a hundred years from now? You will be alone and unhappy, and when you decide your life is no longer worth living, it will be too late because you can never die again."

He opened his lips to speak, but closed them.

"You chose another woman because of obligation. It was your choice, your mistake," Elide said, "but that is what we do. We make mistakes, and we have to live with them. Don't think you can escape it without consequences."

Seraphine nodded and took a step back. "A wise one you are, dear girl."

As the swarming ocean surrounded them, all Theon did was grip Elide's hand, and they soon opened their eyes to find themselves embracing each other in the midst of the dark forest.

Violet put down her pen after the last period. "I finished it Wyatt," she said amidst tears welling up in her eyes. "I finished your story."

*   *   *

ALONE IN THE ROOM, Violet sat in front of the canvas. She twisted her onyx colored hair now lightly streaked with gray. She reached up and brushed the last stroke of color onto her painting.

She took a couple steps back, admiring her artwork.

"A young man embracing his lover in the midst of a dark forest," she said, to no one in particular. She had relayed those words every day for the past ten years.

Violet eyed the couple in the painting for some time. Shades of prussian, ebony, and ash enveloped them, and yet couldn't mask their vibrant love for one another, their fiery passion.

"This is my best work yet." She set down her paintbrush.

She was startled as the door burst open, two children entering.

"Mother!" the little girl cried, carrying her little brother. "Wyatt is crying."

Violet rushed over to her daughter, Charlotte who was struggling to carry her little brother. Violet lifted Wyatt out of Charlotte's arms.

"There, there," she whispered. The boy's crying began to cease.

Charlotte peered around her mother, looking up at the finished painting. "Mother," she said. "It's so pretty. What is it?"

Wyatt rested his head against his mother's shoulder.

Violet turned around. She smiled, extending her arm so Charlotte could grab it. "It's a story, Charlotte dear."

Charlotte jumped continuously. "Oh, I love stories. What's this one about?"

Violet's eyes went from her daughter to her art work. "Love that lives for all eternity."

OUR LOVE
By Vy Le

I don't know why I fell for you
But it happened so quickly
My heart skipped a beat
when I saw your smile

The most beautiful thing I've ever seen
It's like sunlight
shining into my dark world
Brings me warmth—
Finally, I can relax.

We usually meet in the music room
Sometimes barely talking to each other
You sit next to the window
Looking outside, enjoying the peaceful time
While I sit in the corner
 playing your favorite song.
You never bother me when I'm with my guitar
You're the only one who's never done that.

Sometimes, you're so annoying
Latching to my side,
hammering me with questions.
I will tell you you're so annoying
But deep down, I love your annoyance
It reminds me that you're still here.

You are my soul, you are my life
You make me feel the warmth
that I thought was lost.
You bring me joy and happiness
You bring me confidence when I feel useless
You're always beside me when I need you the most
I love you, I love you
More than anything in this world.

THE JOURNAL
By Michelle Nguyen

The journal
So covered and completed
With hundreds of characters and scribbled thoughts
And phrases and quotes
And taped images and memoirs

The journal
Is a place where every small mark
Holds meaning
The drag of a letter
Is the frustration that causes
The ruining of a perfect line

Oh, how each page is covered
In scribbles
Like his wrists the night before
Family time

And notice how he saves a page
Solely for his thoughts after each month
And how it is messily written upon
You can picture his anger
Turning against the sensitive paper
And it crumbles and smudges

I asked him
Wouldn't it be easier to talk?
To speak up?
Than to hide behind pages and
Explode onto paper
With no reply back

He uses no color
No, each doodle whether it be
Flowers or cars
It is drawn in black ink or with gray graphite
In class
Beneath his binder
As his eyes look up every so often
In worry of getting caught

I wondered what the stars
Meant to him
They were everywhere
In the corners of every page
Used to decorate every blank spot
Perhaps he knew

Perhaps he knew
That he would become one with the constellations
Shining and finally showcasing
His bright smile in the sky
He has no body
No, he prefers it if only his smile
Was left to admire

I set his journal back down
Safely next to the unopened casket
And join those who have gathered
We are dressed in black
Hoping to somehow resemble the night sky without city lights
For him to find his way home
And shine once more

MOON AND STARS
By Vivian Tang

When the night comes
You rise up into the heavens
You're the rabbit that's been captured by a fox
A maiden trapped in the celestial being

We are untouchable
But, you know I'm here for you
Wherever you may be throughout the day
I'm endlessly spinning around you

Our memories shine like the stars
I close my eyes to avoid all the feelings
But you shine brighter than the darkness that is me
Beautifully filling up the night sky with light

Faint memories fall like the stars
While others twinkle brighter than the sun
You are the heaven that I will always treasure
While I am the earth who can never have you

DEFIANCE
By Christine Do

ERIN LEANED BACK IN her revolving chair, casually sipping from her cup of green tea. Her computer screen casted a dim orange glow against the darkened walls of her dorm room. She waited for news of her recent "achievement" to be broadcast on the Internet.

She grinned as a notification popped up on her computer. She clicked open the article and a news video pulled up as she scrolled through its transcript. A reporter stood in front of Expo Labs, which housed one of the many research databases for microchip manipulation sponsored by the Supreme Council. The six powerful individuals called the Supreme Council, oversaw Earth's transformation to the modern world of Techna. Council members made promises to the people. True, they did deliver incredible technological advances to the citizens, but at what cost? Microchips, which altered the entire genome, were now implanted in babies born to those whom the Supreme Council considered to be exceptional humans.

"This is by far one of Recode's biggest break-ins, having set back the research being done here by months," said the anchor. "Expo Labs' data is currently being analyzed for further information, but it is suspected that this is the work of Recode's most famous Hacker, Melody, who has yet to be captured. Citizens are uneasy about the recent events that have occurred, and the Supreme Council is working hard to find this Hacker and bring the rebellion to an end. Any information on the elite Hacker has yet to be discovered."

Erin scoffed. Of course they had no information on her, the current leader of the decade-long Recoder resistance. As an elite Hacker, she used a voice changer and a face mask to cover up visual and voice recognition and always made sure to wear gloves to cover up her fingerprints. This was child's play, but it was not without risk. If a Recoder was caught, he or she would be either executed or wired into software and programmed into a Sentinel, the assassination super soldiers who were under personal control of the Supreme Council. Erin was about to turn off the computer, but the anchor piqued her interest by announcing an important message from the Supreme Council. The video transitioned to Sean, the leader and spokesperson of the Council. Adored by the unsuspecting public thanks to his charming looks, charisma, and sophistication, Sean sat in a plush red armchair in his office at the Council headquarters.

"Melody," Sean said, "is one of the greatest Hackers Recode has ever had—the greatest inspiration for the rebels. If Melody is caught, the Recode's base will fall entirely, and the citizens of Techna will finally live in peace without such," his face contorted as if he ate something bitter, "*nonsense* in our streets."

Erin's ego had already inflated when classmates commented on how she could be the first female Supreme Council member because of her high class ranking, but for a Council member to think that she, the coder known to everyone simply as Melody, had such importance to the Recoders—made her heart swell with pride.

"So we have proposed something special for our citizens."

Erin paused, pulled out of her grandeur daydreams, and leaned closer towards the screen.

"The person who finds and turns in Melody will be rewarded with great power." The chairman smirked, causing Erin to scowl. "That person will obtain the very power me and my fellow chairmen hold. Whoever turns in Melody will become a part of the Supreme Council. Even those of you that are part of the Recode are welcome to join this grand chase as you please."

Erin gasped. Her phone lit up from the barrage of notifications from her fellow Recoders. She quickly shut it off as she waited for the chairman to continue.

"To my dear Melody out there, I suggest you watch yourself from now on. Or maybe—" the chairman paused, a smug look etched on his face, "turn yourself in now before it gets ugly."

She unplugged the computer and buried her face in her hands.

Erin had no classes to attend tonight. She moved her cursor to open her messages so she could interact with her fellow Recoders like she usually did, but then hesitated. Instead, she changed Melody's status to invisible to other members; any messages Melody read would not be 'seen' by others.

The more Erin read, the more her heart sank. They discussed how turning her in would give them leverage, reasoning that with inside access to the Supreme Council, the Recoders could attack when least expected.

It wasn't a shock that Jax, a self-proclaimed "best Hacker," lead the topic. Half of the people online sided with him, seeing the sacrifice of Melody more beneficial. Others were unsure that surrendering such a talented Hacker was the best gamble. It wasn't that Jax and the others disliked Melody; while she was an extremely capable Hacker, it was safer to turn her in in hopes that she could infiltrate the Council and destroy it from within instead of potentially being captured and turned against the Recoders, as a precaution, as Jax explained.

Erin sighed, rubbing her temples. Everything she had worked for was falling apart. Her parents had passed away when she was young, leaving behind a moderate sum of inheritance. Utilizing nothing else but her knowledge of technology amassed over years of studying, she earned a spot in her university and, as Melody, became the strongest Hacker in the Order of Recode. Now, she could even create her own brand new tech, such as a metal cuff that gave her access to any mainframe database with a touch and an access code. She used it to insert a virus that would corrupt the Council's computer records. It only took her ten minutes to hack into Expo's lab. She was the secret weapon in this game, yet the other members were still willing to throw her out. They had the audacity to speak of her as some disposable pawn.

Erin spent the rest of the morning pacing back and forth in the small, cramped dorm filled with stacks of open books and blueprints scattered on the floor. *How could this be happening? I don't have a way out of this. Unless…*

She turned to her computer and began typing as she dove into research. As meticulous and outrageous this plan was, it could end the game. Whatever hours, days, weeks, years put into this would all be wasted should she be caught. Her typing slowed as she weighed her risks again, then picked up at a faster pace. If she had to gamble with her life to free her people, then so be it.

She sat back reading over the outlines, satisfied with the result.

"They told me to watch out?" She scoffed. "Oh, wait till they see…"

Erin packed her stuff into her backpack and headed out the door.

The world had transformed into the modern cities that the people of the 1900s predicted. Buildings were tall and sleek with futuristic lights. Cars could hover and fly. But Erin trusted none of it.

Once on the streets, she could hear the tune of a street band playing the same melody she grew up listening to when her family was alive. She stopped for a second hiding herself among the crowd and concentrated on the familiar song.

When she was content, she left for morning class at Lux University, the song still ringing in her ears.

* * *

It had been nearly eight years since the Supreme Council first publicized the reward for Melody's capture, but all that came up were clear fakes that the Order of Recode had sent. Melody became more and more discreet with her defiance to the Council. It was reported by one of Council's spies in the Recode that Melody was no longer working for or against them. The rebellion had simmered down for the past years without their top Hacker, resorting now to small hit-and-run attacks.

Sean huffed as he listened to his fellow councilmen speak; Kade, Simon, and Malcom much too adsorbed in the conversation to notice the annoyance on his face.

"We need Melody under our control to finally put an end to all of this," Kade said.

"We could just arrest another high member of the Order—" Simon began to say.

Malcom cut him off. "We can't. Recode is a complicated organization. Only Hackers can tell us what is really going on, and Melody is the key to all of it. She saw through our plan straight away. I don't understand why she would align herself with a group of foolish human beings."

"Enough." Sean rubbed his temples. "This talk getting us nowhere, and it's giving me a headache."

"Would you like me to get you some tea, sir?" a girl behind Sean asked. The men in the room turned to the her.

He nodded at the girl, thanking her with a sweet smile as she left the room to get him his drink.

"Who's that, Sean?" Simon asked.

"That's my new assistant, Erin. Though I usually don't take help from anyone, her record was beyond extraordinary."

The councilmen leaned forward, wanting to hear more.

"Erin's records in dealing with our chips showed that she understood the material beyond many of our scientists. I believed that she could be useful in helping us find Melody. If we can connect her to our software database and keep her under our control, she could possibly counteract what Melody does. We could have her infiltrate Recode and possibly get more information from them. With the help of the other spies we have, she could potentially pull the information we need to bring down Melody and the Recoders once and for all."

The men nodded and waited until Erin came back a few minutes later, carrying a tray full of tea cups for each of the gentlemen. When she was sure they had each taken a sip, she headed for the door, bowing on her way out.

"Wait, Erin," Sean said. The girl stopped with her hand on the door. "Yes, sir?"

"Stay here." He pointed to the Sentinels. "I want everyone who isn't a councilman out of this room."

Erin backed out of the way as the Sentinels guarding the room walked out past her in unison, locking the door behind them. The girl walked toward the table of men, stopping to stand besides Sean.

Kade, who sat across from Sean at the other end of the table, explained their plans for her infiltration of Recode, and how she would be a great asset to the takedown of the Order. As he finished, he gestured at Erin. "So what do you say? Will you take the risk for the sake of Techna?"

Erin tilted her head. After a while she answered, "I'm sorry. I'm afraid I can't do that."

The Council stared in disbelief at the girl. How dare she deny an order from the Council? This was treason of the highest degree.

Before anyone could speak, she continued, "I'm afraid that I'm already on my own mission." A faint smile appeared on her face.

Within seconds, the Council members were restrained at their wrists and ankles by shackles to the chairs they sat in.

"What is the meaning of this?" Sean said, gritting his teeth as he pulled against the bonds.

"Hmm? For such a group of geniuses, you couldn't put two and two together? Well, I guess you were right to say that I am quite the cunning person then."

Kade furrowed his brows. "You're Melody, aren't you?"

Erin giggled with a glint in her eyes. "Bingo."

Simon struggled in his restraints. "You and your Recoders are fools. Every one of you. You have no right to defy us. We are the ones in charge, the ones in power. You live freely under our Council, and yet you disobey—"

Erin slammed her hands on the polished redwood table, her coy expression turning into one of anger. "Freedom? What freedom? Your power is corrupt! Can you not see that the people only follow you because they are brainwashed? You aren't leaders. You alter minds to get your way. You kidnap people to make them mindless guards."

Sean laughed. "Let me guess, one of your family members had become one of our Sentinels?"

Erin looked away, tears beginning to form.

"No? Or perhaps… did your family member die?" His face twisted into mock sadness when her face fell. "I've looked through your records, Erin. Your mother died in childbirth despite our technology, and your father had joined the Order of Recode to seek revenge, but it wasn't worth it in the end, was it? He became a Sentinel and then a Guard of Recode killed him. This is why you're fighting us? Oh child, you really are juvenile aren't you. You're a part of the group that killed your father."

Erin's jaw tightened as she glared at the man. "How did you know that? I erased it from my database."

"That was in my memory actually. I was there that night when your mother died. It was back when we were testing new medical technology; your mother's death was merely a flaw in the system."

Erin dug her nails into her fists; unshed tears threatened to spill over the edge of her eyes. Sean took this moment to continue.

"When you applied for the company as one of Lux University's top students, I was quite intrigued… A programming major applying to be an under-glorified secretary. Did you think I wouldn't notice? I've been watching you since then. Why else would I have allowed you to set this room up so you can reprogram the chairs to cuff us?" The cuffs unhooked, releasing the Controllers' hands. Sean lunged from his seat, pinning the stunned girl to the wall. Erin struggled a bit in his grasp, but one hard slam into the wall sent her strength rushing out of her.

"You are smart, but not *that* smart," he said, bringing her hands together with one hand and gripping her chin so that she was looking at him in the eyes with the other. "You have potential to become much more than you are now. You just need a bit of… reprogramming."

Erin looked him in the eye. "Why did you let me do what I did? Why did you allow me to be Melody if you knew who I was?"

Sean's words were cold. "I didn't realize you were her until I had your background checked when I first decided to hire you. You are a genius beyond comparison and everything you are able to do was reflected in Melody's work. Do you think we don't know how Recode works? I'm surprised as how foolish you are. You walked right into our hands."

"But Malcom said—"

The aforementioned man came up to lean against the wall besides her. "It was all a play, little girl."

Erin furrowed her eyebrows. "That doesn't answer why you allowed me to become your assistant if you had my background checked and realized who I was."

"I hired you to confirm that you were Melody. The results were just as I predicted. You are the key to everything, and you just threw yourself at us." Sean cackled in her face.

Erin felt the blood rushing into her head and growled. *Anything but… this.* With her remaining strength, Erin leaned back and swung her head into the man's forehead, causing him to step back, releasing her from his grip. Malcom moved to grab her arm, but she kicked him in the face. His head smashed against the wall with a loud thump. One of the Council members pressed a panic button, alerting the Sentinels outside who moved in to restrain the girl.

"Disgusting." She threw in a last kick before the Sentinels swarmed her. "All of you corrupt, abhorrent, horrible—"

The Sentinels gripped Erin like a vice. Tears fell as she struggled against them.

Simon walked towards the thrashing girl. In his hand was a device that Erin knew was used to reprogram the algorithm of the microchips embedded in every human at birth. "On your command, Sean."

Sean picked himself up and dusted off his suit. Erin would have laughed at the redness on his forehead if not for the dire situation.

He bent down in front of her. "It's the end of the line for you, sweetheart. Any last words?"

She became still, simply looked up, and smiled.

Sean flinched as he heard a cup crash to the floor. "What?"

He turned to find the other councilmen fall one by one. Sean felt weaker, falling to his knees. The Sentinels released their grip on Erin as the Council fell in defeat.

"How?" Sean's voice was quiet and hoarse.

Erin stood before the dying councilman.

"A Hacker never reveals her secrets." She took one last look at him before she kicked him down to the ground, knocking his last breath out of him.

The girl walked over the bodies of the now deceased Council members towards the large window in the room that gave her a view of the Capital of Techna. She picked up the cup of tea that one of the councilman drank from, swirling the contents of the cup to reveal the nanomachine packets in the tea bag. She had programmed them for a delayed release of poison once they had been ingested and circulated around a body. The Council were doomed the moment they drank the tea.

Erin went to a nearby monitor and tapped several keys to immediately halt the Sentinels' directive. They would need to reprogrammed, or rather, unprogrammed. Other Recoders would take care of that, and she would be there to help.

Erin looked down on the street. Down below she could hear a familiar faint melody of music by the usual street musicians.

The triumphant Hacker gazed at the view of the city, content.

It was a new age for Techna.

COMING HOME
By Clarisse Tran

Careful not to fall too far in
Keep a close watch, put life into perspective
These habits need to be corrected

Light resides, however,
Through the tangled vines of despair
There's still a part of you there

Days have passed and the time has come
Swim out of your dark woods
Let go of your fears

Have you forgotten the fun
The beauty once there and the spirit so kind
Overflowing with light, you and I intertwined

Release the pain and bring back the life
The person I knew
I know it's still you.

A New Chapter in Life
By Alvin Nguyen

We were once strangers
You didn't know me
And I didn't know you
You sparked a conversation
But it only lasted for a short duration

As time goes on
We began to bond
You are no longer a stranger
You became my life changer

You gave me light
You gave me hope
You are the reason I shine so bright

With all of my might
I shall fight for you
Even if it's the last thing I do

CHANGED

By Kelly Ho

I feel your heart is different
The way you look away
I know that you've stopped caring
Though you would never say
You stopped saying that you love me
You don't smile when I call your name
Our meals are filled with silence
And the sound of your phone games
You've stopped loving me
Just say it to me straight
Don't make me be the bad guy
Don't make me say these words
'Cause I'm still the one who loves you
Though your heart has long moved on
And I still remain.

NO WOMAN MORE THAN SHE
By Aithy Nguyen

Tell, oh tell, why you say that there is no woman who can compare,
there may be one more fair than she
> *I beg to differ, for there is no woman more beautiful than she*

There may be one more honest than she
> *You are wrong, good sir, for there is no woman more true than she*

There may be one more strong than she
> *And I say not, for there is no woman as mighty as she*

There may be one more talented than she
> *By no means are you valid, for there is no woman who can do as much as she*

There may be one more honorable than she
> *Never, for there is no woman as righteous as she*

There may be one more kind than she
> *You are wrong yet again, for there is no woman as selfless as she*

There may be one more brave as she
> *Indeed not, for there is no woman as courageous as she*

There may be one who can love more than she
> *And tell, oh tell I say, there is no woman whose love can fill as she.*

I Don't Feel Good

By HongAnh Nguyen

I don't feel good.
There's a ringing in my head,
An aching on my side,
There's something on my mind.
I don't feel good.

My hands are getting sweaty,
My forehead's getting spotty,
There's something on my mind.
I don't feel good.

Was it what I ate this morning?
Maybe I'm not drinking enough water.
Perhaps I've fallen ill.
There's something on my mind.
I don't feel good.

Could it be in my head?
Have I made up a sickness?
What if I'm actually fine?
There's something on my mind.
I don't feel good.

Now that I think about it,
Perhaps it was you.
Your smile that brings butterflies,
Your laugh that brightens the damp sky.
Perhaps it was you.

With that cute eye smile,
And that awkward grin,
It was you on my mind.
I don't feel good.

INCOMPLETE
By Emily Tran

IT WAS LIKE ANY other day. I woke up, brushed my teeth, got ready for school and left to catch the bus. It was a day like every other. Boy was I mistaken. When I got home from school, I sat on my bed, homework spread out all across my bed. There was a knock on my door. I looked up to see my dad opening my door.

"That's weird," I thought, "Dad never comes home early."

Once I saw my dad's face, I was concerned but remained silent. He looked solemn, but nevertheless walked toward my bed and sat down. He pushed my homework out of the way, took my hands in his, and took a deep breath.

"Hey, Buttercup," my dad greeted me with an attempt at a smile. "Something happened today with your grandma."

My heart stopped, dropped, rolled, doing anything you could think you of. What was he talking about? I saw her this morning and she seemed fine.

I looked up, trying to meet his eyes. After figuring that I was unable to, I settled to stare out the window next to him.

"What happened, Dad?"

He sighed in response. "After your grandma left today, she was going to drive to the store but..." He dropped his gaze. "Someone ran a red and hit her car, Sweets. She...she's gone."

Tears started to pool in my eyes. My heart clenched. I remembered my mother's close relationship with my grandmother.

"How's Mom?"

"That's what I wanted to talk to you about, Lily," said my dad. My heart raced. "Your mom is taking this really hard right now, and I know you have school and everything, but we're going to need an extra hand around here."

I nodded my head. "Yes, of course, Dad."

Over the course of the next few weeks, the pace at which my mom deteriorated was faster than I expected. I watched her fall apart at every single thing that reminded her of my grandmother, which was practically everything considering how my grandmother was always over at our house. My family had tried to keep each other in check, of course, just to make things easier for my mother. But she wasn't who I thought she was anymore.

My mother started coming home later than normal, her breath reeking of beer or cheap liquor. She became less and less loving. She became quick-tempered, letting small things such as dishes on the table and socks on the floor make her angry.

One night she just snapped.

It was a Thursday night. I was doing homework when all of a sudden I heard screaming. I jumped up from my bed and ran down the stairs, and there she was yelling at my little brother. He spilled a small cup of water on the otherwise immaculate table. My brother, close to tears, scooted back as she took steps towards him. I ran over, covering my brother.

"Mom! Stop! It's fine. It was just an accident. I'll clean it up," I said.

My mom's glare hardened. "How *dare* you stop me like that? *I'm* the parent. Get out right now. I'm trying to teach your brother a lesson," she screamed.

I picked up my brother. Ignoring her, I walked toward the stairs, but my mom blocked my way, her eyes blazing. I put my brother down and gently coaxed him up the first couple steps. I could tell he was scared of my mother, because at this moment, this wasn't my mother; this was a stranger, a monster. My mom raised her hand over her head and started to walk towards me as I walked backwards. Slap! Her hand collided with my face before I could even blink.

"Don't ever undermine me ever again," she said. "You understand me?"

Tears gathered in my eyes, and I nodded my head without hesitation.

"Clean this mess up and get out of my face." She walked out of the house and got into her car, probably to buy more beer. My brother, who was glued to the stairs during the whole ordeal, ran to me. He hugged my legs and sobbed. I sat on the floor and took him in my arms and we cried together for the woman we could no longer call Mom.

After this event, my brother and I spent every moment we could out of the house, whether it was doing homework at the library or me watching him play soccer. And when we were home, we tiptoed around my mother, never waking her from her drunken sleep and kept to ourselves in our respective rooms. I could tell as much as my father loved my mother, he was also at a loss at what to do, so he started to avoid coming home too, spending as much time at work as possible in order to keep busy. Weeks passed before my dad came into my room again, and when he did, remembering what happened last time, I prepared for the worst.

"Hey Sweets, how was school today?" he asked

"Fine, I guess," I muttered.

He sighed. "Lily, I know these past few weeks have been hard with your grandmother and your mom and having to take care of Jacob more often, but you know it's only because she's grieving."

"And she thinks we aren't?" I said, standing up from my bed. "I'm so sick and tired of grieving alone, Dad. Mom should definitely not be grieving alone, either. Look where that got us."

My father looked down to his hands. "I know, baby, I know. But that's not what I came in here to talk to you about," he said. My eyebrow rose, indicating for him to go on. "Your mother got let go from work today."

You could hear the echo from my palm hitting my forehead and I groaned. "Mom, why…" I said under my breath with my eyes closed and fingers pinching the bridge of my nose.

My dad went on. "She hasn't been going in to work these past couple months, and they were making cuts, almost completely forgetting she even worked there. They didn't hesitate to cut her seeing as she was absent for an extended period of time," said my dad. "I know this is a lot to take in, and I'm being selfish to ask you for more, Lily, but we can't get behind on the bills, you understand?"

I sighed, knowing exactly what he was talking about. It was inevitable, now that I thought about it. I was getting a job.

After applying for several jobs, I started working at a local department store, about a ten-minute walk from school. It was owned by a nice elderly couple who were happy to let me work for them despite my small stature. It was a new routine to get used to. Every day, wake up, get ready for school, walk Jacob to school, then I go to school, and right after school I walk to work, and after work, I go home to do homework.

A couple weeks passed when, despite this being my established routine, my mother confronted me one evening after I got home from work.

"Where have you been?" she said. I could smell the beer off her breath from a mile away. "You were supposed to be home hours ago."

I rolled my eyes, so fed up with her at this point.

"I was at work," I said.

"Work?" asked my mom, "You don't work. Don't you dare lie to me. You're too lazy to work."

I clenched my fists and my jaw. I snapped my gaze back to my mom.

"Are you really saying that to me, right now? Have you seen yourself, Mom?" I said. "You *lost* your job. Why do you think I had to get one? Someone has to help Dad keep food on the table." I could tell at this point that my mother was seething, but I dug on anyways. "Because of you, I now take care of Jacob, I help feed our family, I clean the house, I garden the yard, and I go to school. I don't

181

even have a social life anymore because of you, Mom!" Angry tears streamed down my cheeks. "But you know what, if I'm so lazy, I guess you don't need me here right?"

I grabbed my bag and ran out the front door in no particular direction. If I had stayed a moment longer, I would've seen the stunned look on my mother's face. But all I could think about at that moment was getting away from that house and that woman I once called Mom. I ran and ran until I just couldn't anymore. I bent over to catch my breath, no idea where I was. I looked up and saw a seesaw and swings and a slide. This place was familiar. This park… it was a part of me when I was younger.

When my eyes and mind cleared up, I knew for sure where I was, I was at the park. My first park—the park where my mother used to take me all the time, the one place where I was always happy, no matter what was going on. I climbed on the merry-go-round and lay down in the middle as it spun. I tried to hold back my tears as I thought about how happy I was before my mom became a stranger in my house. I was drifting in and out of consciousness when my phone rang. I jumped and picked it up. It was my dad asking where I was. I told him I was fine and that I would be back in the morning and not to worry.

The next morning, I woke up and checked my phone. It was 8:00 A.M.

I scrambled up from the merry-go-round and ran home. It was Saturday, which meant Jacob had soccer at 8:30. I ran through the door, calling for my brother, except he wasn't there. No one was home, except my mother of course. I walked into the kitchen and saw the note my dad left saying he left to drop off my brother at soccer practice.

My plan was to stay home that day and ignore my mother. When I walked in the living room, I was met with a sight I wasn't expecting. Instead of my mother being passed out on the couch with a bottle in her hand and a frown pressed onto her face, she was awake, and sober. She was looking at our family albums with tears streaming down her face. With every page she flipped, a new tear fell. I walked towards the stairs. When I was about to step up, my mom called out to me.

"Lily?" she said.

I froze. The soft, tender voice I hadn't heard in months broke the silence. Not knowing what to say, I grunted. She motioned for me to walk over to her. I approached cautiously, just in case my mother decided to raise her hand again. She patted the seat next to her. I sat down slowly, bewildered by her behavior. We locked eyes.

"I'm sorry," she said, breaking our brief eye contact.

"Oh please, I doubt that," I sneered.

"I am, Lily. I really am." My mother fiddled with her hands. "What you said to me yesterday it…it really made me think about these past few weeks. How I was treating you all…my children, my husband…I've been horrible to all of you these past couple weeks."

"Months." I coughed.

"Months." She wiped the corners of her eyes. "But I want to get better. I want us to be a family again. I want to hug my children and my husband, something I should've been doing when we were supposed to be grieving together, not alone."

I looked up at my mother and saw the sincerity in her eyes. But as I reached out to grab her, to hug her, the past couple months came back in flashes across my eyes, and I flinched back. I scoffed and stood up abruptly.

"I'll believe it when I see it," I said, moving towards the stairs. My mother didn't move to follow me.

"I will make it up to you, Buttercup," she said.

I flinched. "Don't call me that." I walked up the stairs never once looking back at my mother.

At 11 o'clock, Jacob and my father came back from soccer practice. Right when I heard the door open, I bounced down the stairs and opened my arms for Jacob to jump into them.

"How was soccer practice, Buddy?" I asked as I pecked my father's cheek.

"It was great," Jacob said. "My coach let me play striker for the first time today and I stole the ball four times, Lily! *Four*!" My brother was bouncing with excitement and sniffed the air. "Did you make food?" I shook my head.

My brother, Dad, and I went to the kitchen to investigate and there was my mom making some bacon, a small smile gracing her face. My father walked in first.

"Hey, Honey." My father took slow, small steps. "How are you today?"

My mom looked up. "Good," she said. "I know it's late, but I figured that you guys might still like some bacon for brunch, yes?" My mom had a hopeful smile on her face.

My father's face broke out into a grin. "Of course." He rounded the corner of the counter to kiss my mother's head. Jacob squirmed to get out of my arms.

"Mama?" he asked in a small voice. Mom crouched. "Are you okay yet?"

She tilted her head to the side. "Not yet, Buddy. But I'm working on it."

Content with this answer, Jacob ran up to my mother and jumped into her arms, just as he had done to me just five minutes before. I stood by the door, hands in my pockets as I tried to shrink away from my family in front of me. I wasn't ready to forgive my mother just yet, but I could see the sorrow in her eyes. I could tell she was trying, but I couldn't confront her yet.

"Lily?" my father called out to me, hoping for any sign that I was ready to forgive my mother. I sighed and shook my head.

"Not now," I said. My dad nodded. I turned to walk back upstairs, but as I was walking I heard my mother's voice grow fainter as she talked about the alcoholics meetings she would start to go to in addition to the twelve-step program to make amends with our family. Maybe my mother was ready to finally be forgiven, but I wasn't ready to forgive her just yet.

A few more months went by, and my mom was recovering. She stopped going out at night, started cleaning the house, and made breakfast again. And I began to become more comfortable once again. Every once in a while, we would say bad puns to each other in the kitchen as she cooked and I did homework on the counter, just like old times. Jacob started cuddling with my mom regularly once again and my mother started sleeping in the same bed with my father once again.

Our family was almost complete; all they needed was me, the last piece of the puzzle, to forgive my mother. Forgive the person that was once a monster. Forgive the person that I didn't know, the stranger. Because here my mom was, the loving, caring woman I knew and still know.

Even though it took me months to get around, the moment my mom said her amends to me and apologized to me, I could truly tell she was sorry.

"Hey Buttercup," my mom said. This time I smiled at the sound of my old nickname. "I'm so sorry for the way I've been acting these past couple of months. The stress from losing your grandmother took a toll on me. As important as your grandmother was to me, I should've remembered that she wasn't the only important person to me. I lost the person who raised me, but that didn't mean you should've lost the person that was raising you too. I know it's not an excuse for the way I've acted, but I want to make sure that you know that I will do everything in my power to make things up to you. You, Jacob, and your father are the greatest things that have ever happened to me and I took that for granted."

After she finished speaking, I rounded the counter, just as my father did when he forgave her, and hugged her, kissed her. Here she was—my mother.

The months after my mother apologized only got better. She got another job, gave Jacob his daily hugs, and I got closer to my mother, even more than before.

Despite not needing a job anymore to help pay the bills, my parents suggested I still keep the job to be more independent and have my own money. I was able to work less hours now that my mom got another job. All my friends welcomed me back as I started to spend more time with them once again.

I had my friends and now my family once again.

I was complete.

RED

By Jennifer Ho

If I was a color, I would be red.
Not the nice lipstick red,
but flaming, dangerous, toxic red,
The type of red that tells you to look away,
The red that engulfs you, that burns you instead.

I despise other hues of red,
Pretending that they are all this and that,
Coated in stains of lies.
But the truth is—
They are just as red as I.

A lighter and opaque red
they seem to be,
Pleasant to the eyes of many,
but rather...
Noxious to my eyes.

RIGHT HERE

By Johnson Nguyen

Best of friends, well, at least that's what I'd say,
But slowly and surely, we'll drift away.
You've made friends, so why am am I still here?
I was the guy who listened and cared.
You only talk to me when you need a therapist,
But other than that, I'm irrelevant.
You visit your friends and never tell me, that's great.
Even if you do, you tell me hours too late.
The more I think about it, the more my face drenches with tears,
Because you're occupied with your life while I'm right here.
Even if you set aside your work just to say "Hi",
I would be sincere with every reply.
Truth is, I miss you, you were always by my side.
We stuck together even through the strongest of tides.
I know even best friends come and go,
However, there will always be a place here for you
In my heart with the memories of all of those years
And if you ever need me—I'll be right here.

COPY
By Karen Phung

Outstanding, amazing, you put on a show
Praised for your abilities to write like a pro
Placed on a higher ranking that no one can outdo
Many wish that they can be as good as you.

But that's not the real you, is it—
So simple, so easy, copy, paste, and submit
What makes you so special, what makes you so different?
I can't tell whether it's yours or someone else's gibberish

You say you're original but I only hear the words of another
In the end you're just one of the replicas, like every other
As if you're original, as if you're unique
When really it's a cover-up, to hide the fact that you're weak

Imitation is a form of suicide
You may be safe until someone uncovers your lies
Foolish of you to repeat another's work
When you could've been a true artist creating the artwork.

WAITING
By Emily Tran

I wander through my thoughts sometimes
I go through years and walk for miles
Through all the memories that have made me smile
As I walk out into the light
Darkness comes to fill my mind
As I sprint through the rain
I feel a small strain
Against my heart as it breaks
My body starts to shake
As tears start to pour
from my eyes, onto the floor
They don't understand
That I didn't plan
For this
I didn't plan to meet her
I didn't plan to date her
I didn't plan to fall in love with her
From good times to bad
Through all the memories I've had
I'm just waiting for the time
When I have finished this long climb.

DEVILED EGGS

By Nancy Huynh

"I PROMISED NOT TO tell anyone, but I guess I can trust you." I twirled my thumbs and struggled to meet his eyes.

"Of course you can trust me." He sat across from me with crossed legs and bright eyes.

I'd never imagined myself in this situation, but meeting with the devil was my last resort.

Around his office were paintings of Greek gods, philosophers, superheroes, and legendary leaders—except, these were not your typical ornate portraits. They were mug shots. Instead of holding his lightning bolt, Zeus was holding his placard. Instead of a red and blue suit, Superman was sporting orange and black. The idea humored me, and I felt more at ease.

"My favorite artist drew those," the devil said, referring to the portraits.

Hoping that I could finish the deal as soon as possible, I forced a chuckle and nodded. The monster in front of me was not who I'd imagined. He was short and chubby; his cheeks flushed with red, and his eyes shone bright yellow. He took his red suit off, revealing a white and navy striped pajama set. I shifted my eyes away in embarrassment. Maybe the devil wasn't the right person for my plan.

He cleared his throat. "So, I'm guessing you're not just here to chat with me?"

"I need you to do me a favor," I whispered, fearing that the heroes on the wall could hear me. I began to second-guess myself, and became wary about my haste in visiting Hell.

"Oh. I'm good at favors," the devil said with bright eyes.

My heart pounded louder in my ears as I organized my thoughts. I opened my mouth, waiting for sound to come out.

The devil leaned in, his mouth spreading into a wide smirk.

"I killed him!" I blurted out before slamming my hand over my mouth.

The devil blinked, and his mouth gaped open and closed. I took that as my cue to continue.

"You see, I work at a restaurant. My regular customer, Edgar, comes in. His wife, Shelby, orders his food as usual. The thing is, he's deadly allergic to eggs." I paused to breathe. "But I forgot and…" My face burned from embarrassment, or from the fact that I was sitting in Hell. Tears ran down my cheek at the memory of Shelby's panic stricken face as she leaned over her husband's pale body.

The devil said nothing.

For several minutes, the room was silent except for my heavy breathing.

"And what made you think I can help you?" he asked.

"Well, I've already visited heaven, and the angels wouldn't forgive me. *'Everything happens for a reason'* they told me." I rolled my eyes.

A bell rang from his office. The devil raised a finger.

"Excuse me, my breakfast is ready." He slowly reached towards a cupboard, opened it, and took out a plate of perfectly boiled, soft, large eggs.

My heart ached while the devil savored each bite of the heavenly white egg. A flashback of Edgar eating his delicious, well-done, fancy breakfast made me queasy.

"You are truly evil." I gritted my teeth.

"That's me!" the devil cheered. He sprang up from his seat to reach for the salt and pepper. "Want some?"

"No, I do not want some." I shrieked, frustrated at his tactics. I stood up.

The devil cleared his throat. "You can't just leave like that."

"What do you want? A goodbye kiss?"

"That would be nice," he mused, "but you need to pay for your visit."

"For what?"

The devil ignored me, and instead pushed the button on his monitor.

"You can come in now," he spoke into the microphone.

"Who can?" I turned my head as the door opened.

An angry man stormed into the room. His eyes pierced through my soul, stopping me from breathing. He moved closer to me, with fists so clenched, his knuckles turned white.

I gulped and forced a shaky smile. "Nice to see you again, Edgar.

FROM ZERO
By Vivian Tang

I know I could've been better
Better than what you knew me to be
I took you for granted
Deceived by Father Time

I know I can't erase our memories together
Or change the tides of time for you and I
I want to start over again
Let's write our story from zero

I want to know everything about you again
Like I couldn't do before
I want to hold you in my arms
And embrace you like I never did

Please come back to me
Believe in me once more
Come back to me like it's the first time
And let's start again from zero

HIS LAST WORDS

By Thanh Nguyen

"I'M GOING TO DISAPPOINT you," he said, "but you already knew that."

His voice echoed through my mind. His words stabbed my heart. Who knew this day would come so soon, where everything would collapse in a flash?

His hands released mine, and our hands drifted apart.

Realizing that everything was about to end, I looked down, desperately trying to hide my tears. We were at our favorite parking spot, a small neighborhood next to mine. It was our spot. The spot where we started and the spot where we'll end. Those memories came flooding back.

I remembered those nights, those nights he would call to say he missed me. We still had a trip to France all planned out. Just for us. The preparation for the trip—the plane tickets, the hotel, and the tours—was supposed to bring us closer, but instead, our conversations became shorter, and we slowly turned into strangers. Lately, when my phone would ring, I always hoped it was him, but it never was.

One night, I finally received what I had yearned for: a call from him, saying he was outside. I remembered how he used to greet me with a smile, but tonight, it was different.

Tonight, instead of a smile, there was a smirk painted across his face—that same smirk he showed me when I revealed our surprise trip to France.

We couldn't say a word, nor were we able to look at each other in the eyes.

After he drove me to our spot, he looked out the window anxiously as if he was waiting for me to initiate a conversation, but neither of us could.

Finally the silence broke as he whispered, "I'm going to disappoint you. But you already knew that."

All I could say was, "Please just tell me," even though I already knew where the conversation was going.

With a deep sigh he replied, "I'm sorry, but I don't think this is going to work out. I have been thinking all week about this and I guess it's time for us to move on."

I was speechless. I realized that this night would be the last night to see him and to hear his voice. I would never again hear that deep, soothing voice that was embedded in my mind.

The night ended as he dropped me off. His car disappeared into the fog. I stood there hopelessly. I had lost him.

I took a long stroll around my neighborhood. While I walked home, my phone rang. I pulled out my phone and saw an email notification. It was a verification email of the plane tickets that I had purchased for us, the two of us. Remembering that smirk on his face, I realized that he never even cared to go, nor did he care about us in the first place.

Even though he was now gone from my life, I was still determined to go to France to travel to a new world, to make new memories.

I logged on the website. When I clicked the final button to refund his ticket, I felt a burden lift off me. I scrolled through the pictures detailing my itinerary—the Eiffel Tower, the Louvre, and Notre-Dame—and I smiled, for the first time in a while.

No longer did I feel disappointed. To be happy, I didn't need him.

I should have known that.

SUMMER NIGHT

By HongAnh Nguyen

One midsummer night,
I awoke to the sound
Of rocks knocking.
A crack at my window.
You were below it,
Asking me to come down.
Spend time with you.
What will we do?
You had no plans.
But we'd spend it together, you said.
That night I spent,
Talking to you.
About trees, about life, about love.
We went down to the river,
And set sail on a boat,
Carrying our hopes down to the sea.
When we went home
And stopped by the field,
You got me, a hand of bishop.
You took me up
The roof I never dared to climb
And told me to lie
Under the big blue sky
To look at stars, but I gazed at you.
How can one sky, fit so many stars?
You said.
How can one person, mean so much?
I replied.
You never had an answer.
Neither did I.
Years have gone by,
You have long gone,
And so have I.
But I won't forget,
That one summer night.

NEMO

By Peter Vu

FADE IN:

INT. HOSPITAL ROOM - AFTERNOON

The sounds of coughing and a cardiac monitor beeping is heard as we take a tour around the hospital room. We see flowers, framed pictures, a clock at 2:10 and a stuffed gray wolf named **NEMO** (Nobody in Latin). **JAY NORACE** (17), a loving and dependent kid who craves intimacy and love, is sitting on a chair next to **AMORETTE HOPE** (17), a beautiful young girl that's dying from leukemia, lying on a hospital bed with wires attached all over her body.

> AMORETTE
> You´re worrying too much about the future Jay. You´ll be fine.

> JAY
> No I won't.

Jay looks down.

> JAY (CONT'D)
> I wanted you to meet my kids, Amorette.

Amorette places her palm on Jay's cheek and brings his face up.

> AMORETTE
> It'll be okay, trust me. I'll be there to watch over you and all of your accomplishments.

JAY

What if I don't succeed? I'm scared
of what I'm going to do when you're
gone.

AMORETTE

You made so much progress of
being sober, please don't get back
into it again.

JAY

I'm mentally weak, you know that.

AMORETTE

You're too- (Coughs)

Amorette drinks some water.

AMORETTE (CONT'D)

Depressing. You need to be happy.

JAY

I can't.

AMORETTE

If you can't live a life with happiness,
then live a life spreading happiness.

JAY

I just want to make you happy.

AMORETTE

Your growth and love in life is all I
want before I go.

Jay immediately stands up from his chair and walks around to breathe.

JAY

> (sadly angry) Amorette, you don't
> understand! I can't grow without
> you.

                    AMORETTE

> Don't say that-

                    JAY

> My heart hurts for you. I have
> nobody else besides you. I don't
> want to see you in a casket, I don't
> want to live a day without you!

                    AMORETTE

> Jay...You can't do this to yourself.
> You need to be strong for me.

                    JAY

> (hopeless) I don't know how to.

Amorette struggles to stand up.

Jay quickly walks over and she drops on his arms.

                    JAY (CONT'D)

> Be careful.

                    AMORETTE

> Everything will be alright. I love you
> a lot. I hope you know that.

                    JAY

> (softly) I love you, too.

                                                CUT TO:

INT. HOSPITAL ROOM – NIGHT

Jay and Amorette are watching *Rebel Without a Cause* on the TV. They're
sharing a blanket together in the same exact spot moments before.

                    AMORETTE

> Don't get back into it, Jay.

                    JAY
What do you mean?
                  AMORETTE
I mean when I pass. Don't go back,
resorting to drugs.

                    JAY
Stop saying you're going to pass.

                  AMORETTE
I'm serious Jay.

                    JAY
I won't, I promise.

Amorette coughs and reaches over to her left and grabs her stuffed gray
wolf, Nemo.

                  AMORETTE
I want you to have Nemo.

                    JAY
No way, you had him since you were
a baby.

                  AMORETTE
I know and I want you to have him.

Amorette looks at Nemo and pets him.

                  AMORETTE (CONT'D)
He was always there for me. No
matter what happens, Nemo will
always be there for you.

Amorette hands Nemo to Jay and he hesitates, but accepts the gift. They
both resume watching the movie.

                                      CUT TO:

EXT. BUS STOP NEAR HOSPITAL – MORNING

MUSIC STARTS. Jay walks out of the public bus with a couple of **irises.**

INT. HOSPITAL – LATER

Jay walks inside the hospital and through the hallways toward Amorette's room. Nobody's there. He panics and quickly finds the nearest **NURSE** who's holding a clipboard.

> JAY
> Nurse, nurse! Amorette, where is
> she? Amorette Hope- She was in
> that room.
> (Points to the room)

> NURSE
> (Checks clipboard)
> She's… She's no longer with us.
> (Pauses and looks up at Jay) I'm
> sorry.

> JAY
> (begins to tear up)
> No, no, she can't be. I was here with
> her yesterday, she was fine.

> NURSE
> She's no longer suffering. She's in a
> better place now.

Jay tries to fight his tears as the nurse rubs his back.

CUT TO:

INT. JAY'S ROOM - NIGHT

A small room that contains only a mattress, desk, and chair. Jay is sitting upward on his mattress while looking at a bag full of pills. He's sobs and repeatedly hits the back of his head against the wall.

JAY
Please, I don't want to do this. I don't. I can't.

Jay holds onto his head and continues to sob.

JAY
I miss you so much Amorette, please come back. You were the only person that believed in me, you were my only friend, you were my only purpose to live.

Jay opens the bag of drugs.

JAY
I'm sorry Amorette, I can't do it anymore-

Jay suddenly stops and looks at Nemo, which is on top of his desk near a framed picture of him and Amorette. He tosses the bag of drugs into the trash.

CUT TO:

EXT. CEMETARY - MORNING

A gloomy morning at a cemetary. From a distance, Jay is seen walking up to Amorette's grave with a couple of **irises** and Nemo. He places the flowers and Nemo near the tombstone plaque that states, "In Loving Memory of Amorette Hope; Nov. 27, 2000 - Feb. 10, 2018"

JAY
Happy Birthday Amorette, you're finally eighteen. It's been nine months ever since you've passed and I've missed you so much. I'm sure you're tired of me saying that all the time, but it's true. I think about you all the time and I don't think I'll ever stop.

Jay crouches down.

                    JAY
      It's been really lonely since you've
      passed. I don't have anyone else
      besides Nemo, but I'm not sad
      about it. I can feel your presence
      every time I'm with him, and I
      believe you're here with me keeping
      me alive.

Jay stands up and picks up Nemo.

                    JAY
      I lived for you Amorette, and I will
      continue to live for you.

Jay walks away.

                                        FADE OUT:

THE BALLOON
By Monson Wilson

A lonely red balloon in the sky
Going up in the air
Flying way up high
starts to fade, while time passes by
The balloon slowly goes down
Losing air without a sound
Drifting away as the wind blows
Flying into a tree, stuck with nowhere to go
A boy finds it and takes it home
Keeping the balloon in his room
Knowing that it will be gone soon

HIGH HOPES

By Nancy Huynh

The balloon popped and out came confetti
Messages and secrets that you wouldn't tell me
Your full name, your address, your phone number, too
There's nothing that I wouldn't know about you
So tell me, my friends
Why do you do such a thing?
To leave your whole life hanging from a string?
Did you think it would fly
Miles and miles away?
I could drive to your place in less than a day.
How embarrassed you'll be
When I tell you the news
That I know your whole family
And the size of your shoes
Would you be mad at the fact
That I read what you wrote?
Or more of the fact
That your balloon didn't float?

Promises Renewed

By Kimberly Nguyen

DIM YELLOW LIGHT FILTERED in through the window from the hallway and projected a rectangular box of light on the white tile floor. From her hospital bed, Ellie watched the dark silhouettes of the staff rush past her room. Dr. Stevens' rounded shadow stopped abruptly outside her door. There was the familiar murmur of his voice followed by mamma's broken sobs.

"Ellie?" A girl, with auburn hair twisted into two braids resting against the shoulders of her yellow dress, stepped into the room.

"Nessa!" Ellie's eyes lit up.

"Happy 4th birthday, little sis," Nessa said. "I have a big surprise for you."

Ellie tossed back the white ironed sheets, exposing her pale legs. "A surprise? For me?" She sat up on her knees.

"Of course. I wouldn't miss giving my baby sis a present on her birthday." Nessa had her hands hidden behind her back.

Ellie reached outward, bouncing on the bed. "I want it. I want it."

Nessa laughed and pulled her hands from behind her, revealing two handmade dolls. "This one is you." She pointed to the doll with short blonde hair and a bubblegum pink dress. "And this one is me." She held up the one with auburn braids and a yellow dress.

Ellie squealed and snatched up the dolls, clutching them to her chest.

Nessa sat on the edge of the bed and brushed a golden lock of hair from her sister's face. Outside the room, the soft murmur turned into a clamor of voices, each trying to speak over the other.

Ellie pointed at Dr. Stevens' silhouette "Nessa? Am I going to die? I heard Dr. Stevens say that I-I have San-Sanf—"

"—Sanfilippo syndrome," Nessa finished for her.

"Is that bad?"

Nessa placed her hand over Ellie's. "It just means that you're a little sick." She looked away. "Mom says you will be all better soon and we can go home and play like we used to."

Ellie's voice was reduced to a small squeak. "I'm scared, Nessa."

Pulling Ellie closer, Nessa wrapped her arms around her sister's frail shoulders. "I am, too." She nuzzled her face into Ellie's hair. "No matter what happens, I'll be right here. I'm going to help you get better…I promise."

"Even if it's scary?"

"Even if it's really, really scary." Nessa tightened her grip around Ellie. "I'll protect you, no matter what." Little did Nessa know that those were the last words Ellie would ever hear her say.

*　*　*

"Night, Nessa." Ten-year-old Eliot waved a hand in the air as he passed Nessa in the hall, his white hospital gown swaying at his ankles.

"Didn't I tell you to call me Doctor Ryan?" Nessa playfully rubbed his head. "What are you doing up? You should be in bed resting."

"I'm doing a little exploring." He shrugged. "The hospital at night looks so different. What about you? Are you working all night again?"

"Don't change the subject, mister. Now, off to bed with you." She nudged Eliot.

"Fine," he said. "Don't stay up too late or you'll get wrinkles."

"Woah, young man. I'm only forty-two," she said, but Eliot had already turned the corner of the white corridor. Nessa shook her head and opened the cream door to her office at the end of the hallway. Inside, papers were strewn across the mahogany desk in the center of the room and large bookshelves towered against the walls. Nessa pulled up her black leather computer chair and shuffled through the papers until she found a large yellow post-it note with an intricate formula scribbled in black pen. Examining the note for a moment, she flipped on the dark computer monitor on the side edge of the desk and continued her research.

"Dr. Ryan." A nurse in navy blue scrubs burst into the office, waking up Nessa who had fallen asleep at her desk. "It's Eliot."

Nessa sprinted down the hallway into Eliot's room. She flung aside the white curtains allowing dawn's light to illuminate the white walls. In the midst of the light she saw Eliot's body sprawled out on the bed, multiple wires hanging from the crook of his arm. As she approached the bed, she saw the sweat that poured from his pale forehead and heard his labored breathing.

"Eliot. You're going to be okay." She ran her fingers through his wet hair. "Look at me. You are going to be okay."

Eliot turned to face her. "I know," he said weakly.

Nessa examined his vitals on the monitors next to his bed.

The nurse behind Nessa changed the a IV bag, and the fluids dripped through the tubing into to his arm. Almost immediately, Eliot's breathing slowed and the color began returning to his face.

Nessa wiped the sweat from Eliot's face with a damp towel. "You really need to take it easy from now on."

"Don't worry, you can't get rid of me that easily." Eliot shot her a weak smile. "Dr. Nessa, you can tell me the truth, I know—"

"Do you remember what I told you when you first came in?"

"That you were going to help me get better. Even if it gets really, really scary."

"That's right, and I'm not going to break that promise okay?" She tightened her grip on his hand. "Now get some rest. I'll be right here with you."

Nessa watched as Eliot's eyes began to droop and eventually closed. His hand momentarily tightened around hers as she lifted her hand.

In the hallway, a nurse was waiting for her.

Nessa wiped tears from the corners of her eyes. "It's gotten so much worse. I'm not sure if he'll survive the rest of the day."

The nurse placed a hand on Nessa's arm. "I'll watch over him. His parents are on their way. You go get some rest. I promise you he'll still be here by the time you came back."

"I just wish there was something I could do. Something…Anything."

"Until someone finds a cure, these kids are in God's hands now."

"A cure…" Nessa's mind raced. *The formula.* "Please watch over him for me." Nessa rushed down the hall to her office. She grabbed the post-it note from her desk and hurried into the lab. She began mixing vials of medicine into a single solution. She pulled the solution up into the syringe and capped it.

Code Blue. Dr. Ryan please report to room 404. I repeat. Dr. Ryan report to room 404, a voice over the hospital intercom said.

By the time Nessa entered the room, there were three nurses and medical assistants hovering over Eliot's bed. In the opposite corner of the room, Mr. Henson, Eliot's dad, held back his wife who was screaming at the staff.

"Save him, please," Eliot's mom said through sobs. "Somebody, please, do something."

Nessa pushed her way through. On the bed, Eliot gasped for air. His white hospital gown was soaked in sweat. The heart-monitor attached to his arm beeped quicker. Eliot's limbs flailed in the air. The hospital staff administered another IV and another injection, but the situation did not improve.

All the while, Eliot's mother's panicked voice blared through the room like an alarm.

The seizure subsided, but Eliot struggled to breath.

"Nothing's working," one of the nurses said.

"There's nothing we can do," another responded. "Doctor?"

Nessa looked down at Eliot. His face was pale as the white sheets he was lying on. Eliot's eyes wide with fear, darted around the room until they rested on hers. Nessa averted her gaze and turned to his parents in the corner of the room.

"Mrs. Henson, there's something that might save him…an injection. But it's still in its experimental stages and I can't promise—"

"Do it." Mrs. Henson sobbed. "Anything to save my baby."

Nessa looked at Mr. Henson who nodded in agreement. Behind her, Nessa could hear Eliot gasping. She pulled the syringe from her coat pocket and nervously uncapped it. Glancing at the nurses, Nessa turned and rolled up Eliot's sleeve.

"It's okay, Eliot. Remember my promise?" She leaned in and kissed his forehead. The entire room went silent as the tip of the syringe entered Eliot's arm.

Eliot opened his eyes to the white ceiling of the hospital room. He turned to see Nessa asleep in a chair by the bed. "Dr. Nessa." He called out to her. "Wake up."

Nessa opened her eyes and smiled. "How are you feeling?"

"Better. My arm kind of hurts though. It's like some old doctor lady gave me the wrong shot." Eliot gave her a devious smile.

Nessa chuckled. "I should have made it more painful."

"Well, at least you kept your promise. Am I cured?"

"For now all of the symptoms of Sanfilippo are gone but we can't be sure." Nessa paused. "Eliot, do you know why I made that promise the first time I met you?"

He shook his head.

"Because I made that same promise to someone very special to me a long time ago. Back then, I wasn't able to keep it. When I first met you, you reminded me so much of her. It was as if I was given another chance to fulfill my broken promise."

"I always knew you would." Elliot grabbed Nessa's hand and gave it a reassuring squeeze.

Nessa smiled, a feeling of peace wrapping around her.

CRUEL
By Kelly Ho

There are times when I wonder
Why life is so cruel
I keep asking myself why
But I know I'll never know

These obstacles, this pain
They say it'll help me grow
But nothing seems to comfort me
Everything still feels wrong

I wonder why I must endure it
Why I must fight these tears
When the world has clearly
Abandoned me leaving me here

They tell me the same old words
Though it no longer has its charms
Why does it seem that the world
Just wants to do me harm

The world just keeps on pushing me
Move on and learn and grow
But how am I to do so when
My heart just won't let go

I loved I lived, and grew within
Thanks to them being by my side
Yet why must the world take them away
Forcing me to say goodbye

Indeed the world is cruel
And life just loves to play its games
They both seem to enjoy watching us
As we cry and feel the pain

But I want to yell and scream and shout
Please stop having me in it
My life was happy sweet and warm
Before you meddled in it

You're evil mean and just plain harsh
I hate you when you hurt me
But I know deep down
That you just want to truly help me

To say goodbye hurts me greatly
But like you said I know I'll grow
But I can't help but hate you
Cause you make my loved ones go

I know you don't want me to cry too much
You want to me to learn to cope
So here I stand sucking up my tears
And holding onto to my last hope

You saved me I know you did
From being hurt later down the road
But I just wish you didn't have to take away
So many that I love

Why can't you help me learn
Through other means and methods
Why must it be that you force me
To send so many to the heavens

I really hate it right now but I'll let it go
And your cruelness I'll forgive
But never do I want to feel
The pain I feel within

THE PAST ONCE HELD
By Thanh Le

Stare into the sky—breathe in the cool, crisp air
Close your eyes, remember past guilts—if you dare
Rather than fall, stand proudly and tall
Act as if you are a person so fair

The rosary fingered an entire lifetime
Holds a heavy past burden
Do you fall victim of the darkness in your heart?
Or on a journey of forgiveness shall you embark

Morning light arises whether you awake
The freedom from guilt that your heart aches
Only if you walk forward may you find a way
To be free from the past, shameful days

Memories fade, true, but never truly lost
Take the reins of guilt's chariot, despite the cost
It's painful to face moments wished to be forgotten
But you shall grow stronger, once you face them

Guilt is no wind that directs your ship east
Every hero's sword can slay any beast
You are the hero, your past—the beast
Forgive, but never forget, so that regrets may cease.

WHAT ARE YOU AFRAID OF? (SELF-IMAGE)

By Kristy Diep

Self

It is the song of broken hearts.
The last breath that you take as water fills your lungs
Not wanting to go up for air
Because air seems like such a distant memory
So foreign to us
We are afraid
Afraid of what might come out of the other side
What you might open your eyes to see
We are blind
Because being blind is so much better than waking up to see the destruction of life
The only thing holding you down
Is yourself.

Image

Shattered into whole pieces,
Each memory,
Floated above the shallow water,
Drained.

Stripped of its color,
Vision blurred,
Focus.

Grip on the past,
Slip within each grasp that had hurt us before
We hold on to that invisible string that we thought had so much value
Afraid,
Afraid of what had become of us.

What we thought was missing
Was actually always there.

BENEATH THE PAINT
By Clarisse Tran

Lips: crimson red
Eyes: drawn long and sharp
Locks: puffed and curled

Too long it takes to cover
Cover the stubble on my chin
Cover the man that's within

Have I made the right decision?
To hide rather than to fight
Because I have not a voice?

But only that fear
Beats through my chest
And drips through my veins

I've decided to hide
Life no longer mine
And that's just fine

IN THE DARK
By Derek Nguyen

"THIS IS RICHARD TRAN to Captain Ambrose. We have reached the LZ."
Richard's headset crackled with interference. "Captain Ambrose, do you read me?"
The interference grew to a droning whine, causing him to wince.

The brush behind him rustled, and a young blonde woman wearing an
ensign's uniform stepped out. "No luck, Richard?"

Seeing him shake his head, she pulled out her scanner and pointed it at the
vegetation. "Biological readings are off the charts. These organisms have new
elements in them."

She knelt down by a bush and picked off a large, ruby berry. "The scanner
says it's edible." She raised it to her lips. "It looks just like strawberries back on
Earth."

He slapped it away before she could pop it into her mouth. "Careful Lana,
the scanner's been known to be wrong before." Richard adjusted the frequency on
his headset, but the static grew louder. "No use trying. Let's get back to the
shuttle." As the two trekked through the dense foliage, the red sun dipped below
the horizon. Within twenty minutes, the entire jungle was draped in total darkness.
There was no light apart from the lamps on their helmets and the neon greens and
blues of bioluminescent orchids hanging from towering trees.

"It's so beautiful here." Lana looked at Richard and smiled. "This is why I
signed up for this." She pointed at the ceiling of vines covered in the glowing
flowers. "To see this."

Richard glanced at a pair of glowing orange creatures that resembled
dragonflies and grunted. "Yeah, sure. Just remember that we're here to locate a
suitable place to start a colony. Sightseeing comes later." He pointed towards a
clearing. "We're almost back. Let's hope Austin and Susanna had more luck
contacting Ambrose."

As they pushed their way out of the towering ferns and stepped into the
clearing, they were greeted by a middle-aged man wearing a grey engineering
jumpsuit. Richard shook his head and said, "Austin, there's too much interference.
I couldn't contact the captain."

"Susanna and I couldn't contact him with the shuttle's coms either." Austin rubbed his grey stubble and looked at his scanner. "I suspect it has something to do with these new elements. They're everywhere, from the rocks to some blue insects I saw earlier. It's going to take a while before any technician can develop something to completely bypass the interference."

The three walked over to a short, cylindrical shuttle where a woman was tinkering with a control panel. Richard coughed to get her attention and asked, "Is everything ready, Susanna?"

"Give me a moment." Susanna shook her head, causing her short black hair to fall in front of her face. She put two wires together, only for a cascade of sparks to fly out. She slammed the panel shut and leaned against the shuttle.

"Damn piece of tin…" Susanna turned to the group and shook her head. "The main power generator is busted. We'll have to wait until sunrise so the auxiliary generators can charge up to full capacity." She looked at the sky. "I knew it was a bad idea not performing a systems check before leaving the mothership. And here I was thinking I would get a hot shower after this." Susanna holstered her tools and looked at Richard. "So what now, boss? We can't leave until dawn."

Lana groaned. "We're stuck here? Can we at least sleep in the shuttle?"

Richard cursed and looked back at the dense jungle. "The shuttle's too cramped, we'll have to sleep outside. Good thing we planned for a situation like this." Stepping into the shuttle, he pulled out some sleeping bags and lights. Walking back outside, he said, "If you want to sleep sitting straight up in a chair or in the tiny cargo compartments, then be my guest. I'll be sleeping outside tonight."

The group took them and established a perimeter around the ship; the dim amber emergency lights casted dark shadows across the ground.

"Susanna," Richard said. "Take first watch with me. We'll swap with Austin and Lana after two hours." He climbed onto the shuttle and sat down, unholstering his photon pistol and putting it by his side.

"Why me? I spent hours trying to fix the stupid shuttle." Susanna stuck her tongue out at Richard and settled down on the damp grass.

He chuckled and turned on his night vision goggles, bathing the jungle in bright greens and hazy whites. Two golden moons rose in the sky, accompanied by twinkling stars.

Austin laid out his sleeping bag by the shuttle and settled in, tipping his visor down. Soon he was snoring. Lana followed suit, lying propped up against one of the shuttle's landing gears.

Susanna sat down near them, pushing two pairs of emergency lights into the ground beside her. "It's so peaceful here, with the natural lights. It's a nice change of pace from all the duties aboard the mothership. But it doesn't have hot showers." Glancing skyward, she smiled. "The night sky is beautiful. Take a look, Richard."

He glanced up at the golden moons and multitude of stars that hovered in the sky. "Indeed it is. Now if the blasted interference went away, this planet would be perfect."

Susanna smirked and peered off into the jungle. Chirping similar to that of crickets permeated the night, supplemented by strange howls and croaks.

Coupled with Susanna whistling "El Mañana," Richard's eyes began to droop, and within thirty minutes sleep draped itself over him.

Twenty minutes later, he snapped awake. In a panic, he looked over the edge of the shuttle. He sighed in relief when he saw Austin and Lana snoring below him, then he frowned. It was too quiet. Susanna always whistled a song as an all clear signal. "Susanna?" Richard picked up his pistol and hopped down, looking around in a circle. Nothing.

He shook Austin and Lana. "Guys, wake up. Susanna's missing." Both of them started and got up on their feet. They activated their headlamps and peered into the dark foliage.

Lana said, "Maybe she's having a restroom break? It could be like that time on Verenus IV when we couldn't find her. You called in rescue teams, and she was exploring a cave the whole time."

Austin grunted. "Susanna wouldn't do that on a night watch. I think something else happened. Look right there. The grass is all crushed, as if something heavy was dragged away."

He followed the trampled path into the forest and motioned for them to follow. There was a trail of snapped branches and torn cycad leaves where a person tried to grab something to pull themself away. They had walked for about a quarter of a mile when the trail went cold. Austin scratched his head. "The hell? It's as if it just vanished into thin air." He looked around at the tree trunks. "Unless she was lifted up…"

Lana looked up at the canopy and froze. Austin looked back at her and frowned. "What's wrong?" She put a hand over her mouth and pointed a shaking hand at the tree above him.

Richard followed her gaze and nearly screamed. In the trees above Austin, there was what appeared to be a reptilian leopard—it's six legs ending in sickle claws. And impaled on its spiked back was Susanna, a permanent scream etched onto her face.

Richard signaled for them to turn off their headlamps, but it was too late. The creature shot a look at the trio and roared. Before they could move, it shot off into the trees. "Turn off your lights and only use your night vision goggles. We can't give our position away."

Lana and Austin complied and drew out their pistols. Austin looked at where the creature had vanished and gulped. "Why didn't we think of the possibility that there would be predators?" He knocked the side of his head and growled. "We can't go back to the shuttle. That thing or other creatures will follow us and pick us off."

Lana gagged and brought up a hand to her mouth. "So you're saying we have to kill it first?" A crunch broke the night silence, and her eyes widened. "Did it…" Seeing Austin's gaunt face, she shivered. "Wait, do you guys hear that? The rustling… I think it's coming closer. It's coming back."

Austin waved everyone back. "Get around this tree. Be absolutely quiet." The three stood huddled together, their ragged breaths the only sound breaking the silence. Richard glanced up at the foliage above them and squinted. Between the green and black he could just make out four white points in the darkness. They vanished before he could take a better look.

He tapped Lana's shoulder, and pointed up. She nodded and aimed her pistol skywards. He followed behind her, with Austin behind him. "See anything?" he whispered. Lana shook her head and pushed aside a cluster of thick vines to circle around the back. Richard raised a hand to brush aside the vines then saw that one vine glistened and had scales. And it was inching towards Lana.

"Behind you!" Austin pushed Richard aside and dived forward. Just before the creature could grab Lana, Austin knocked her away. In a flash, the creature's tail wrapped around his torso, whisking him up. It slammed him onto its back, stabbing him on the spikes. Screams tore apart the silence as Lana and Richard opened fire, their pistols launching blue bolts at the creature. It roared as the shots burned its reflective black scales, and the reptile jumped into the darkness.

Richard turned to Lana and grimaced. She whimpered and began sobbing. His chest contracted, and he vomited on a tree. Austin's screams still echoed across the canopy. As they faded away, they could hear him crying for help in the darkness. There was a sickening crunch, and the pleas stopped. Richard grabbed Lana and ran. "We have to get back to the shuttle. Now."

Branches whipped against their face and thorns tore into their skin. Lana stumbled over a rock and yelped. Richard lifted her onto his shoulders and began carrying her. "Come on. Just a little bit longer." A roar boomed across the canopy. "No, not like this." Looking around, he spotted a tree with sprawling roots. Putting Lana in between them, he said, "I'll distract it. When you hear me open fire, get to the shuttle and lock it. Don't open it. Not even for me."

Lana shook her head, but Richard had already dashed off into the brush.

Climbing onto a tree branch, Richard peered into the dense blanket of vines and glowing orchids. The night vision goggles created strange apparitions among the shadows. Apart from his deep breaths, there was no sound. Hearing soft rustling, he peered across the canopy and neighboring trees. Nothing.

The dead silence became a constant drumming against his ears. In the corner of his right eye, he saw a tail shoot upwards. Richard inched further out to look for the creature. A drop of saliva dropped in front of his face, and he leaped sideways.

The reptile pounced onto where he had been standing, a horrifying white ghoul under the night vision. He could still see remnants of Austin's and Susanna's uniforms between its teeth. Grabbing a vine, he swung over to a neighboring tree and fired at it. Blue bolts whined through the air and burned into its shoulder. It growled and leaped across the canopy, evading his shots. Richard cursed as the pistol overheated and burned his hand.

While he was distracted, the creature jumped at him, swiping its claws at him. He stumbled as they grazed his chest, the force sending him tumbling off the tree. Richard pulled himself into a roll and sprawled on the ground. As he tried to rise, sharp pains pierced his left leg as teeth sunk into it, then his back burned as he was flung into a tree. His pistol flew into the bushes, and he drew a knife. "Dammit all!" The reptile growled and stepped forward, raising a clawed foot.

Before the creature could disembowel him, a burst of photon bolts slammed into its side. "Run Richard!" Lana stumbled forward, firing her pistol at it. "I'll hold it off." He struggled to his feet and limped over to his pistol.

Hearing a scream, he turned around to see Lana get knocked onto the ground, streaks of crimson blood flying from the slashes caused by the reptile's claws. It leaped forward and clamped down on her hand, wrenching it clean off.

Richard picked up his pistol and aimed at its eye. The handgun kicked back and a bolt burned through its upper eye, pierced its brain, and then flew out the other side in a puff of azure blood. It reeled back in its death throes and collapsed on the ground with a low gurgle. Its scaly chest heaved once, and then the creature went silent.

Richard hopped over to Lana and began applying first aid. "Dammit, why did you do this? It would've killed you." He reached for a med kit on his utility belt and smeared some foul smelling foam on the slashes and the stump where her hand was. She grunted in pain and shook her head.

"I couldn't let you die." She made a pained smile. "Besides, I'll get a shiny metal hand now. Just like in all the sci-fi movies." She gasped as the medical foam burned into her flesh, forming an opaque film around the wound. Richard wrapped a dressing around it and lifted her up.

"Don't talk, save your strength. The medicine should keep you stabilized. You lost a lot of blood." The reptile's corpse glistened, and he glanced skyward to see the red sun peek over the horizon. "Let's get back to the shuttle. You'll need immediate medical attention and three months' leave at least. This mission went to hell, didn't it? Austin and Susanna…dammit."

The two staggered into the clearing and got into the shuttle. As the generators were charging, their headsets crackled again.

"This is Captain Ambrose. What is going on down there? We've been trying to contact you for hours. Only now did we get a signal through."

Richard wiped the sweat off his head and looked at the two empty seats behind him. Turning on his communicator, he grimaced and said, "Austin and Susanna are dead, sir. I'll explain along the way. Long story short, this planet is far from being ready to be colonized. Far from it. We're going to have to step up our efforts if we want to avoid the hell me and my crew went through." Lana gave a thumbs up, and he powered up the engines. With a low rumble, the shuttle rose off the ground and shot off into the blue sky.

A SHIP ON ROUGH SEAS
By Kimberly Nguyen

A small ship tossed in the waves,
Ripped from the shores of sanity.
Their lives at the mercy of God,
Himself, small and insignificant.

The crashing of waves against the bow,
Beating and breaking the weak.
Any attempt to regain control,
Is thwarted by the force of the sky.

Oh, how seemingly insignificant
Our lives seem now, when a small
Weather-torn ship winds up on the shores
Its inhabitants long forgotten.

REALIZATIONS OF A SELF-PROCLAIMED TEENAGER

By Kristy Diep

When,
A son whines at 10 p.m. about curfew
From the distraction of games
That brainwash his intestines
Filled with curses and rhymes,
Verses and crimes,

The daughter crops her shirts
Because of a boy from English class,
An attention seeking app,
The flesh
She left to be revealed
Maybe this will help her be healed.

We are all sufferers of the world's
First problems,
Eighteen
Being legal to vote but can't shake
The responsibility
That rides along in the
Passenger seat.

What controls us

Coming home at 3 a.m.to
Blue lights
And the dark room
In which the media still echos
Behind the screens
In our minds.

The balance and imbalance
Levels of dopamine and
Serotonin
That is an uncontrollable
Reaction that
Wires us off the rails
Empty trails
With an uncertain path
On what's to come.

THE INDISPENSABLE LIST OF CHICKEN NAMES
By Thanh Le

THE MOST POPULAR CHILDREN'S bedtime story in Lunara goes as so: once upon a time, there was a witch in the woods who captured an unsuspecting maiden with short black hair and shining blue eyes. The witch took the maiden up to Argew Mountain. At the mountain's summit, the maiden's pure heart and the light of the blue moon gave the witch incredible power. She built a palace made of blacker-than-black stone, ivory pillars, and the bones of her enemies. Every year since then, the witch continued to kidnapped maidens. Countless dashing knights, nobles, and even peasants, have tried to venture to the top of Argew Mountain, only to be met with defeat and failure.

As another blue moon approached, the people of Lunara fear that another maiden would be stolen and the witch would become unstoppable. Perhaps one day someone shall be able to defeat the evil witch and bring safety to Lunara once again.

* * *

"Did you hear?" a villager whispered. "Penelope was kidnapped by the Evil Witch of Argew Mountain while she was fishing at the river."

"How terrible," another villager said. "Her sister must be so devastated."

"This must be the witch's fiftieth maiden. First, the blue moon approaches and now this. Surely, the end is near."

The villagers continued to whisper amongst themselves, fretting about their inevitable doom.

A young girl parted the crowd. A boy her age followed closely behind her. The villagers hushed when they recognized Mabel, the sister of the kidnapped Penelope.

"I'm going up to Argew Mountain." Mabel had a backpack in hand full of bread, cheese, and other traveling essentials. "You're going with me, Noodle."

"What? Why me?" Noodle, her best friend, sputtered. "You want *me* to go up to Argew Mountain? First of all, you know that there are hundreds of monsters roaming outside our village, right? And that the witch is the most wicked lady to have ever existed? And—"

"Listen Noodle, we call you Noodle for a reason." Mabel punched his shoulder. "How about you do something useful for once in your life?"

"You don't have to go that far." Noodle sighed. When Mabel roped him into doing anything, it never ended well. Regardless, he still would agree to participate without fail every time. *I guess that's what childhood friends do for each other*, he thought. "Let me go home to pack."

"Don't have to. I already packed for you." Mabel held up a filled backpack.

Noodle's eyes widened as he took it, but when he held the backpack in his hand, his eyes narrowed. He examined the bag to see if anything was amiss. When he was sure that there were no bombs or poisons in the bag, he followed Mabel out into the forest.

The villagers saw the two teenagers leave without a sound, and as usual, they whispered to one another. The pair could see the jet-black Argew Mountain, miles away, piercing the sky. Clouds of a dark gray coiled like snakes, discouraging anyone from approaching.

There, the castle sat as a conqueror would on his throne.

"I'm surprised you want to go save your sister, since you two don't get along too well." Noodle enjoyed the forest scenery before him. Light trickled down through the emerald foliage, kissing the ground. Birds sang a splendid melody. It had rained in the forest recently, so the petrichor enveloped him.

"One, we get along just fine," Mabel said. "Two, I'm not going to save her. I'm going to beat up that evil witch for choosing to take her instead of me." Mabel gripped onto her backpack tighter mimicking the same emotions she felt when she discovered Penelope was gone. "How dare she think that Penelope has a purer heart than me. Why should Penelope be the fiftieth maiden? She doesn't deserve to kick start the Apocalypse. She's not that special."

Mabel looked towards Noodle, seeking validation, albeit with a glare.

Noodle broke into a sweat thinking of an answer, refusing to meet Mabel's eyes. He stared behind Mabel and concentrated on a spider waiting on its web for its prey.

"Maybe she's using Penelope to lure you into a trap?" he lied. Everyone in a fifty-mile radius knew that Penelope was the sweetest girl in all the lands. She was the type of girl who would offer a hungry fawn her lunch, even if it meant she would go hungry for days. Mabel on the other hand...she was something else.

"You're absolutely right," she said. "That witch knew I was too strong for her. Wow, Noodle, you really can use your head, huh?" Mabel gave a triumphant smile. She broke into a skip, humming a song about how she was the strongest girl in Lunara.

"At least we can save the world by doing this." All Noodle could do was let out a sigh of relief.

The two journeyed for several days in peace. The witch's monsters, which they had been told roamed the land, were nowhere in sight.

"How strange." Noodle tapped a finger on his chin. "Why do you think we haven't seen any monsters on our journey?"

"They're probably afraid of us," Mabel said without even turning her head.

Her ego really is something. Ah, at least it gets us through. It's endearing in a way, Noodle thought while they continued to walk.

On the dawn of the seventh day, the two reached the base of Argew Mountain. A small campsite-like area greeted them. Merchants in their white tents tried to sell wares to those brave and naive enough to try to face the witch.

"This shield can protect you from any magic blast," Merchants yelled. "This sword can cut the witch in half! This potion can heal any wound!"

"This place is a scam," Noodle whispered to Mabel and snickered.

"This place's full of liars." Mabel scanned the area, counting how many people were in the camp.

Many injured knights were in the hands of healers—their groans echoed throughout the camp. And yet, despite it all, the morning sun still rose, illuminating everything in a lavender light. Daybreak was trying desperately to fight the darkness of the mountain.

"Since the end is so close," Noodle said, "people must be trying their hardest to fight the witch and save the world."

"I suppose they all failed," Mabel said. "How pathetic."

Noodle smiled reluctantly. "They're...trying their best."

From up close, the mountain was a citadel of black. The dark gray clouds danced dizzyingly—making it difficult to see through. Noodle shivered at the sight, while Mabel stared at the path leading up the mountain. She gripped her backpack tighter and began her ascent.

"Let's go Noodle. It's time we finish our quest."

"R-right." Noodle followed behind her.

The path up Argew Mountain was full of twists and turns, ups and downs. Signs littered the path; red, bold letters created phrases such as BEWARE and YOU'RE NOT WANTED HERE. Noodle walked at a rapid pace, holding his arms close to his body and constantly scanning his surroundings. Mabel led silently, always looking forward. At every sound, be it a squirrel rustling bushes or a raven cawing, Noodle flinched. After the thirteenth time, Mabel turned around.

"Stop being such a noodle, Noodle!"

Mabel yelling at him made him yelp in surprise. "Hey, it's scary over here. It's perfectly fine to be scared in a place like Argew Mountain."

"Don't worry about it. If something comes, I'll protect you." Mabel turned back around and continued to hike.

Noodle was stunned for a few seconds before yelling, "Hey, wait for me."

Crossing through caltrop traps, cliffs with narrow paths, and various types of shrubbery, the pair finally made it to a clearing. There, they were met with five black chickens with red eyes, grazing on the fresh, green grass.

"They're so adorable." Noodle walked up to a chicken to pet it.

"You know, it's about time for lunch," Mabel said.

"Don't you dare, Mabel." He glared at Mabel. "Look at this one. It has a cute little white heart pattern." Noodle poked the heart.

In that second, the chicken let out a ferocious screech. The other four chickens took notice, and rushed to their screeching friend. The four circled around their friend, clucking a tri-tone in sync.

Noodle and Mabel gasped. This was the song that past soldiers heard before their demise. They could only watch. Their feet felt like lead. They wanted desperately to flee in the other direction, but they could only stay to see the show. Dark clouds surrounded the chickens, and when the clouds faded, a giant, black chicken stood. When its eyes locked on the pair, it let out another thunderous screech, shaking the nearby foliage. The two had to cover their ears with their hands as the chicken cried, and cried, and cried. When it finally ceased, it charged at the two—like any predator would to its prey.

"Noodle, watch out!" Mabel grabbed her paralyzed friend by the arm, dragging him away from the chicken's path. The chicken barely missed pecking him, cracking the ground with the force of its peck and sending rocks flying. The chicken let out a rumbling cry when it turned around.

Noodle shook his head. "We're going to die. This is it. This is the creature of the apocalypse."

"I have a plan." Mabel shook like a fawn as she rummaged through her backpack. "On the count of three, you run that way, alright?" She pointed at a narrow gap between the rocks.

Noodle nodded and prayed for his legs to move.

Preparing its charge, the chicken kicked the earth.

"One."

Its beady eyes locked in on the two.

"Two."

It began another charge, letting out another screech.

"Three!" Mabel took out an orb from her backpack. She threw it at the chicken's legs and it burst, releasing white smoke.

The chicken, not wanting to make any contact with the unknown substance, backed away. It tried to peck the smoke, seemingly in fear for its life, but it was only met with air.

Mabel and Noodle ran into a narrow pathway where the rocky cliffs blocked any sunlight.

"I knew you brought bombs. I'm surprised you didn't put it in my backpack, for once." Noodle laughed, hitting Mabel's shoulders lightly.

Mabel shrugged. "You wouldn't know what to do with them anyways."

"I'm not that useless." Noodle crossed his arms, turning his head away. He glanced around and shivered. "It's chilly here."

Mabel peered further down the path. "It looks like there's a clearing ahead."

At the end of narrow pathway, an open field greeted the pair. The sun poked through the clouds, scattering patches of light all over the grass. Noodle stood in one of the sun patches, instantly warming up. He smiled and opened his arms, embracing the sunlight. Mabel stood in the shade to his right.

Many small cottages dotted the area, with the one in the center being bigger than the rest. Hundreds of chickens filled the fields, though this time, they were white and brown.

"Is that Penelope?" Noodle pointed to a girl feeding the chickens congregated in a single area. His eyes widened "It is."

"Eat, my children." Penelope smiled as she threw grain to the hungry birds and laughed when the chickens chased the flying grain. Her white dress flowed in the wind, and the sun's rays kissed her light brown hair.

"Penelope." Mabel stomped through the mass of chickens with Noodle following silently. "What are you doing?"

"Ah, Mabel. It's…great to see you." Penelope forced a smile, as she backed away a little bit. "What are you doing here?"

"I was here to beat up the witch for taking you." Mabel jabbed her thumb at herself. "If she wanted a maiden with a pure heart, she should have taken me."

Penelope's smile disappeared. "That's why you're here?" Penelope wrinkled her nose and turned away with a huff. "You're not here because you wanted to, I don't know, save your sister from the so-called evil witch? You're not here because you were concerned about my well-being?"

Noodle wanted to ask what Penelope was talking about when she called the witch "so-called," but he decided that fading into the background would be a better choice. However, he was pleased to see that Penelope standing up for herself, so he showed her a thumbs-up. She gave a small smile in response.

"Penelope, what are you talking about?" Mabel arched her eyebrows. "You're not making any sense."

"I don't understand how Noodle has tolerated you this long. You're awful Mabel, don't you know? You only think about yourself. So that's why I came here: to escape from you."

Mabel was stunned. Her eyes widened, trying to comprehend her sister's words. When she opened her mouth, an old woman with a cane and a fair girl with bright blue eyes and short black hair appeared next to Penelope, from a cloud of purple smoke.

"Let's play, Penelope. You're done feeding the chickens, right?" The girl jumped around Penelope. "Oh, who are these people? Are they also maidens?"

"She's Penelope's sister, and I'm their friend," Noodle said putting his hand up.

"Oh, hello, I'm Laya." Laya hopped up and down. "Everyone around here likes to call me Princess Laya, though."

"You got past our guard-chicken, Devilla?" The old woman put a hand on her mouth. "My, my, that's impressive. You two are the first. Welcome to our home."

"Wait a minute," Noodle said, squinting at the old woman. "Are you the Evil Witch of Argew Mountain?"

The question shocked Mabel out of her trance.

The old woman looked at Noodle. "Is that what they call me? My word, they can't even be bothered to use my name, Pox?"

"Of course that's what they call you. The stories say that you're going to end the world on the night of the blue moon." Noodle raised his arms in disbelief.

"That's not true at all." Laya puffed out her cheeks. "People have been making up bad stories about my Grandmother, haven't they?"

"It's all because I'm ugly, isn't it? My graying hair, my wrinkled skin, my triangular nose, and my hunched back, all of those make people think I'm some evil witch. I'm just trying to have a chicken farm with my granddaughter." Pox crossed her arms and sighed. "What else did you hear about me?"

"Your evil monsters roam the land," Mabel added. "Which after what I just saw might seem to be—"

"Lies. My only magical creature is Devilla, and she watches over the mountain, since pesky people always try to bother us."

"She tried to kill me." Noodle trembled as he recalled his near-death experience earlier.

"Oh, she wouldn't have. She may have injured you immensely, but she doesn't have the heart to kill." Pox placed her hand on her heart. "She's such a nice girl."

"That doesn't make me feel any better." Noodle lowered his head.

"If you are not an evil witch, why do you kidnap maidens?" Mabel narrowed her eyes.

"I don't kidnap maidens. I invite them to come up and live up here," Pox said. "My beautiful granddaughter Laya was so lonely up here, so I wanted to bring her friends."

"A lot of girls are sad because they're forced to marry someone, or their family is mean to them," Laya explained. "So we bring them here to escape it all. Let's see, Edna was betrothed to a man ten years older than her. Daphne's mother always made her do chores. Omelet was repeatedly proposed to by some snobby knight because she was beautiful, which by the way she is. Well, those are only a few examples. They can always go back if they want to, but no one ever has."

Mabel shifted her feet as she looked away from Penelope, who started twirling her hair and whistling.

"Everything we know about you are all lies," Noodle said. "It's unbelievable. Rumors and stories can do so much damage."

"That's true, but it's no matter to me. The opinions of others are irrelevant." Pox gave a hearty laugh as she extended her hand. "How about you two stay the night?"

"We'll accept your offer. Thank you, Miss." Noodle smiled and shook the witch's hand.

"Aren't you a charmer? It's alright. I've already accepted that I'm a Ma'am."

It was nightfall. Everyone was sound asleep, except Mabel, who walked out to the field to gaze upon the blue moon.

"Today was the day the world was supposed to end," she said to herself. "I wonder how it's going down at the bottom of the mountain."

"Are you cold out here?" Penelope sat next to Mabel. "I brought a blanket."

She tossed the blanket onto both of their legs. They sat in silence, staring at the moon and stars. The full moon illuminated the land.

"I'm sorry," Mabel said, breaking the silence. "I didn't really realize that I was that bad of a sister."

"I know. You're kind of stupid." Penelope chuckled. "But now you know."

"What do you want to do now? Do you want to go back home, or stay here? It's your choice." Mabel couldn't meet Penelope's gaze, so she started counting the stars above.

"That's not something I can easily answer. I love my new life here. Not to be rude, but our village was terribly dull, wouldn't you agree?" Penelope let out a sigh.

"You can say that again. Noodle and you were my only source of entertainment."

"Also, I still can't fully forgive you for all those years," Penelope forced Mabel to make eye contact. "You're an extremely mean-spirited person, to both me and Noodle."

"Did someone call my name?" Noodle flashed a smile and took a seat besides Mabel.

"We're just talking about how mean my sister is," Penelope said.

"She isn't *too* mean," Noodle gave an anxious laugh. "She's just, sometimes she's a little conceited and self-centered, but it makes Mabel, well, Mabel."

"Noodle, you're too nice." Penelope laid back on the grass— gazing at the stars and the blue moon. "You're the only person who tolerates Mabel at this level."

"Still." Mabel also lay back on the grass to face the sky. "I want to try to treat you both better. You two are the only people I like, anyways."

Noodle laid down as well. "That's going to be a challenge for you. All my life, I've only known you teasing me."

Penelope and Noodle laughed as Mabel pouted.

"For now, let's just look at the blue moon. They don't come around too often, you know." Penelope pointed upward.

* * *

The new children's bedtime story in Lunara goes as so: Once upon a time, the world didn't end after the blue moon. Instead, the witch, who was most definitely unstoppable now, chose not to attack, for reasons unknown. Perhaps she was building an army, or invading another land. Some bold storytellers even believe that the witch was slain by the two teenagers who ventured up the summit the morning of the blue moon. Those two never did come back down, after all. But if she was slain, where were the maidens? Many have attempted to venture up the mountain to find the truth, but Argew Mountain remains impossible to traverse.

And so, dozens of different tales about the witch spread across the land. The people of Lunara still hold on to the hope that, one day, a hero will rise and save them from the fear of the unknown. For now, they'll whisper amongst themselves to spread rumors and lies.

STRANGERS
By Tony Truong

She took everything I had to offer, but I would've given it all anyways,
When we played at the park as kids I knew she was special,
Her smile captivated me—I stole glances whenever I could,
Maybe this is why I wanted to be the reason for her smile,
What does falling in love feel like? This must be pretty close.
I wish her happiness—she'll never know
When I see her I only think of memories we've shared,
But that is all they are now—memories
How did it end up this way?
We used to know each other's habits,
to finish each other's sentences,
to have conversations without a single word,
We shared something pure and real,
And suddenly—we were strangers again.

REALITY LEAP

By Kelvin Pham

FADE IN:

INT. UNDERGROUND SUBWAY STATION - EARLY MORNING, TUESDAY

TOKYO, JAPAN

Distorted music plays, as if it's on reverse. We hear a muted sound of a subway pulling into a station. A bell dings again, and again, and again.

The picture fades in. In front of us, we see a line of people in formal business attire by a subway train underground. They seem to be waiting for the doors to open so they can get in. All of their faces cannot be seen because of the glaring light of ivory white that hangs over them. However, we can only see every detail of only one face and that is our protagonist's.

The protagonist, **CAL**, wears a dark raincoat over his school uniform: a white dress shirt, navy blue pants, and gray shoes.

The distorted music continues to play as CAL begins to talk.

CAL (V.O.)
My sister has died 100 times.

The doors open. People flood out and in. Everyone is moving except for CAL. As we get a closer view of CAL, we see that he is on his smartphone. He presses down the buttons and apps with great force. Something seems to be bothering him.

CAL (V.O.) (CONT'D)
Everyone says that I must be making this up. But believe me when I say this...

Momentarily, CAL is the only one standing outside. CAL, without looking up, heads into the subway.

INT. THE SUBWAY - DAY

As CAL sits down, we get an even closer view of CAL's face. He sits by himself from the crowd.

> CAL (V.O.) (CONT'D)
> I can distort reality to my very own choosing.

EXT. THE SUBWAY STATION - DAY

We get a shot of the subway leaving the station. The subway speeds off and there is a close-up shot of its wheels turning.

INT. THE SUBWAY - DAY

CAL anxiously goes through all of his messages in his phone. In a closeup view, we see texts from his sister ("Where are you???" "I can't find you…" "I don't understand why you are doing this to me…").

> CAL (V.O.) (CONT'D)
> With my powers, I tamper reality, like a time-traveller would with time. (sighs) Except, I don't go back and forth in time. Instead, I create a parallel universe, hoping that someday I can bring my sister back from the grave.

The distorted music stops abruptly.

EXT. THE SUBWAY - DAY

The subway comes to a sudden halt and a faraway shriek is heard. Someone has died.

SMASH CUT TO:

INT. A PHYSICS CLASSROOM - 8:00 AM, TUESDAY

The classroom is roomy and quiet. It is a typical Japanese classroom: all students in their formal school uniforms, a chalkboard and podium up front, and large windows on the right. CAL sits at the back near the window while his sister, **NORA**, sits in the center of the front row. Her long, onyx hair and pale skin stands out from the rest.

As the physics teacher, **MR. MORLEY**, a 60 year old man wearing a sweater and a formal suit underneath, draws arrows and waves near two dots connected by a line, the students are busily writing down everything on the board and lecture. However, a disturbed CAL is fixated on his sister.

> MR. MORLEY
> In quantum mechanics, if the electron is small
> enough, it can actually be at two places ...
> at the same time.

The students are in awe. CAL sighs.

> MR. MORLEY
> This phenomenon is called superposition.

MR. MORLEY finishes his drawing and NORA stands up.

> NORA
> Mr. Morley, can I go to the restroom?

Students giggle.

> MR. MORLEY
> Well, this is the third time of the day, Nora.

> NORA
> But this time, I have to go...

One student, **AIDEN**, cackles.

> AIDEN
> Are you serious Nora? You're such a silly
> girl! Stop using the restroom so you can
> cry all you want.

CAL stands up.

> CAL
> Oh shut up, Aiden. Nora has enough!

> CAL (V.O.)
> This conversation has occurred before. It's happening again.

> AIDEN
> Aww, how sweet. A brother standing up for
> his own sister. Please continue ...

MR. MORLEY
Aiden! Cal! I request that you stop this
fighting!

Tears stream down NORA's eyes and she walks out of the classroom. CAL runs
out of the classroom after NORA. MR. MORLEY appears unfazed.

CAL (O.S.)
Nora, wait up!

AIDEN
Aren't you going to stop them, Mr. Morley?

MR. MORLEY
(sighs) I will teach them a lesson soon.

SMASH CUT TO:

INT. THE SCHOOL HALLWAYS - LATER

A weeping NORA is running until CAL'S voice calls out for her. She comes to a
stop. CAL finally reaches her, but he is out of breath.

CAL (V.O.)
If you haven't connected the puzzle pieces yet,
Nora is my sister who, in many realities, dies.
I suspect her death is very soon, here at school.

NORA
Cal, what's going on? Why did you run after
me?

CAL
Nora, you have to listen to me.

NORA
About what?

CAL
(regaining his breath)
Nora, this place isn't safe. You have to run
home. Call Mom, if you want. But just get
out of here.

                                    NORA
                                    (teary)
                    Cal, I don't understand why you're saying all
                    of this to me.

                                    CAL
                                    (yelling)
                    Go, Nora! Go!

NORA nods her head and runs away. As CAL regains his breath, a dark figure
walks behind him. CAL looks back to see nothing. Cal shoves his hand in his jean
pocket for his phone and pulls it out

CAL turns on his smartphone to find text messages from a NORA of another
reality ("Cal, he's after me").

                                  CAL (V.O.)
                    I received Nora's message a couple of hours ago,
                    when I was in a different reality.

CAL then receives a message from an unknown phone number. The text reads, "I
have found you."

                                    CAL
                                (muttering to self)
                    No, this can't be.

CAL looks at the text again and realizes that the person has not finished texting.
More messages appear, but they are blurred out. CAL squints his eyes, but he
cannot make out the letters.

                                  CAL (V.O.)
                    Someone from another reality must be sending
                    me all of this. This could be the murderer.
                    This can't be Nora because this isn't her
                    number.

CAL closes the messages and turns off his smartphone. A hapless CAL leans
against a wall and sighs.

                                    CAL
                                (muttering to self)
                    If this goes as planned, then Nora should be
                    alive by the end of this day.

A high-pitched shriek sounds. CAL immediately turns around and runs down the hallway and takes a couple of turns.

CAL
Nora!

A muffled noise of a fight is heard.

NORA (O.S.)
(yelling)
Please, someone, help me! Stop! Stop!

CAL continues to run down the hallway, but cannot find NORA anywhere. He goes in the direction that NORA left him but to no avail.

CAL
Nora! Where are you!

As CAL turns to a stairway, he sees his sister, now a bloody corpse.

CAL
(despondent)
Nora …

A dark figure lurches behind CAL and raises a hammer behind CAL. Before CAL can even turn around and see the figure, the hammer strikes him and CAL falls to the floor. Everything fades to black.

A VOICE
You have failed. Please try again.

CUT TO:

INT. A PHYSICS CLASSROOM - 8:00 AM, TUESDAY

Everything's the same as before. However, this time, instead of writing anything on the chalkboard, MR. MORLEY walks around with a small book on his hand. He reads an excerpt of Newton's *Opticks*.

CAL takes a brief glance at AIDEN, who has his head down, sleeping and audibly snoring.

CAL (V.O.)
What the hell is going on … I thought parallel realities are supposed to mimic each other.

236

> NORA
> (stands up)
> Mr. Morley, I need to leave.

> MR. MORLEY
> What for, Nora?

> NORA
> I am supposed to leave for choir. We have a
> competition today.

> MR. MORLEY
> Oh, I forgot! Yes, Nora, you may leave.

NORA leaves.

> CAL
> (stands up)
> Mr. Morley, I have to leave, too.

> MR. MORLEY
> What for?

> CAL
> I have to talk to Nora about something.

The class except Aiden laughs.

> MR. MORLEY
> Well, hurry up. You don't want to miss today's
> lesson, do you?

CAL runs after NORA.

INT. THE SCHOOL HALLWAYS - LATER

CAL finally catches up to NORA, but slams into NORA. CAL drops his phone
on the floor.

> NORA
> Cal! What are you doing here? You know I'm
> going to be late to choir.

> CAL
> (breathless)
> Nora …

As CAL regains his breath, NORA picks up his phone. The messages catches her attention, and she goes through CAL's text message. She sees her messages but finds out that she doesn't remember sending them.

> NORA
> (confused)
> Cal, these messages from me … I don't remember sending them.

> CAL
> Nora, I have to explain something to you.

Silence.

> NORA
> Okay, Cal, I'm listening.

> CAL
> (sighs)
> You're supposed to be dead.

> NORA
> What do you mean?

> CAL
> Someone is out there to kill you.

> NORA
> I don't understand. Stop fooling with me. I need to get to choir.

> CAL
> Nora, I'm serious.

A tear rolls down his cheek. She realizes how desperate Cal is.

> NORA
> So, you really believe I'm going to die?

> CAL
> Yes.

                    NORA
          Why are you saying this?

                    CAL
          I'm not the Cal you've known before …
          I'm Cal from another reality. I have the
          power to leap from one reality to another
          reality. But in all of the realities I've been,
                    CAL (CONT'D)
          you've died, and I'm trying to break that
          cycle. Nora, please, some entity is out
          there to kill you.

                    NORA
          Cal, why haven't you told me you were this
          "reality leaper" before? How is this even
          possible?

This thought shatters NORA completely. NORA turns away from CAL. NORA
needs a few seconds for this to sink in.

CAL sees a dark figure spring behind NORA.

                    CAL
          Nora, it's here!

                    NORA
          Where?

CAL looks around for an opening.

                    CAL
          Nora, follow me!

CAL grabs NORA's hand and leads her out of the hallways.

                    NORA
          Where are you taking me?

                    CAL
          Outside!

                                        SMASH CUT TO:

                    239

EXT. OUTSIDE OF THE SCHOOL BUILDING AND THE PARKING LOT - LATER

CAL still has a firm grip of NORA's hand. CAL stops to see if the killer is nearby. They head for the mostly empty parking lot.

Nearby, a Prius starts and follows the kids.

CAL and NORA are halfway through the vast parking lot when CAL trips on a rock. NORA stops.

NORA

Are you okay?

CAL

Nora, you have to go!

Before NORA gets a chance to run, a Prius slams into her body.

CAL

Nora!

She falls to the ground in slow motion and a loud thud is heard.

A VOICE.
You have failed. Please try again.

DISSOLVE TO:

INT. A PHYSICS CLASSROOM - 8:00 AM, TUESDAY

An exhausted CAL is back in his classroom for the third time. At his desk, MR. MORLEY is playing around with a Newton's cradle.

CAL
(buries head on table and slams fist)
Damn it!

He looks up to find no one is actually paying attention to him. He finds that NORA is not at her desk.

CAL (V.O.)
She must have left to the choir thing.

Under the table, CAL turns on his phone and looks through his messages from his sister. "Cal, I think I'm being followed." "Cal, please come outside, I need to see you." "CAL, WHERE ARE YOU"

CAL has an agitated and despairing look. He suddenly receives messages from an unknown phone number. "You can try all you want …" "But you can't save Nora no matter what."

CAL
(stands up)
Mr. Morley, I'm going to leave …

CUT TO:

INT. THE STAIRWAY - DAY

CAL has lost his sister and his mind. He is about to have a mental breakdown. He climbs a couple of steps before collapsing on the stairway. No one is around to see his pain.

He turns around and sits on one of the steps. He contemplates.

SMASH CUT TO:

INT. THE SUBWAY - DAY (FLASHBACK)

QUICK FLASH. CAL, holding NORA's hand, leads NORA into the subway. Before they can sit down, a bullet breaks through the window and strikes NORA's head. Her body drops.

A VOICE
You have failed. Please try again.

EXT. THE SCHOOL'S ROOF - DAY (FLASHBACK)

QUICK FLASH. CAL reaches the edge of the roof and looks down for NORA. He finds her lifeless body on the floor, as if someone pushed her off the roof.

A VOICE
You have failed. Please try again.

INT. THE STAIRWAY - DAY (PRESENT)

BACK TO PRESENT. CAL buries his head between his two hands and begins to sob.

241

INT. THE SWIMMING POOL AT THE SCHOOL'S GYM - EARLY
AFTERNOON (FLASHBACK)

QUICK FLASH. CAL finds NORA's body down and floating in the pool.

> A VOICE
> You have failed. Please try again.

> CAL (V.O.)
> It's not fair…

INT. THE SCHOOL CAFETERIA - LUNCH (FLASHBACK)

QUICK FLASH. CAL is eating lunch with NORA. NORA enjoys her meal until her head falls completely face down into her bowl of rice. Someone has poisoned her.

> A VOICE
> You have failed. Please try again.

> CAL (V.O.)
> No matter how I try…

INT. CAL'S CAR - NIGHT (FLASHBACK)

QUICK FLASH. CAL and NORA get hit by a speeding truck at an intersection.

> A VOICE
> You have failed. Please try again.

> CAL (V.O.)
> Nora still dies.

DISSOLVE TO:

INT. THE PSYCHOLOGIST'S OFFICE AT SCHOOL - AFTERNOON

We see CAL lying down on a recliner. His worn out, red eyes suggest that he has been crying. The door opens slowly to reveal CAL's psychologist, **DR. HAYES**. The doctor enters, carrying a clipboard and sits down next to CAL.

> DR. HAYES
> Good afternoon, Cal. I am Dr. Hayes, your
> Psychologist.

> CAL
> Dr. Hayes, how did I get here?

> DR. HAYES
> You had a mental breakdown during your first period.

> CAL
> I don't recall that …

> DR. HAYES
> Don't worry about that for now. You're here
> to get better, right?

> CAL
> Where's Nora? I need to see Nora …

> DR. HAYES
> Nora left. She came by this morning.

This hits CAL hard.

> CAL
> Why, Dr. Hayes?

> DR. HAYES
> She wanted to see if you're okay. That's all.

Silence. CAL gazes into the light above and zones out.

> DR. HAYES (CONT'D)
> Cal, don't stare to long into the light. It'll
> hurt your eyes. Now, we are going to begin
> your therapy session. I'm going to ask you a
> couple of questions and you will give me a short
> response. Do you understand, Cal?

CAL nods.

> DR. HAYES (CONT'D)
> Okay, first question: Why are you in pain?

Silence.

> CAL
> (taking a deep breath)
> I don't know, Dr. Hayes.

DR. HAYES jots down a couple of notes.

> DR. HAYES
> Do you know what the pain is?

> CAL
> I do, but I don't want to say.

DR. HAYES continues to jot down some notes.

> DR. HAYES
> Now I want you to place your hand on your
> heart.

CAL places his hand on his heart.

> DR. HAYES (CONT'D)
> Think of someone special…someone that makes
> you secure and warm. Think of that person as
> you breath in and out.

CAL breathes in and out. He thinks of NORA.

SMASH CUT TO:

INT. HOME - CHRISTMAS EVE 10 YEARS AGO (Flashback)

A young CAL walks down the stairs to find NORA by the Christmas tree, opening her gifts early. CAL walks by NORA and NORA turns to CAL. She puts an index finger over her lips.

> NORA
> Don't tell anyone, okay?

> CAL
> Of course, I won't tell, Nora. Is this
> going to be a secret between us?

NORA nods. CAL clasps his arms around NORA.

> CAL (CONT'D)
> I love you, sis.

> NORA
> I love you, too.

INT. THE PSYCHOLOGIST'S OFFICE AT SCHOOL - AFTERNOON

DR. HAYES examines CAL like a passionate sculptor upon his best work. CAL wakes up. The glaring light is still on him.

> CAL
>
> Dr. Hayes, Nora died because of me, right?

> DR. HAYES
>
> What do you mean?

> CAL
>
> It's all my fault…

> DR. HAYES
>
> Cal, it's no one's fault.

> CAL
> (stands up)
>
> I have to go.

> DR. HAYES
>
> Cal, sit down, please.

CAL slams the door open and leaves.

> DR. HAYES (O.S.)
>
> Cal!

MATCH CUT TO:

EXT. THE PSYCHOLOGIST'S OFFICE AT SCHOOL - LATER

CAL walks out of the office and heads to the hallways.

INT. THE SCHOOL HALLWAYS - LATER

CAL glances around.

> CAL
> (yelling)
>
> Nora, where are you?

A dark figure darts up the stairway. CAL immediately chases after it.

MATCH CUT TO:

INT. THE STAIRWAY - LATER

CAL struggles to maintain his pace up the stairs.

> CAL
>
> Hey, stop!

CAL stops to pull up his smartphone. He texts his sister. "If you are still at school, NORA, meet me at the school's roof. I need to see you."

CUT TO:

EXT. THE SCHOOL'S ROOF - LATER

CAL swings open the doors to the school's roof. He clenches his fists.

The dark figure, staring into the sky, leans over at the railings at the edge of the building. CAL heads up to the figure and places his hand on the figure's shoulder. The figure turns and reveals itself.

The figure is AIDEN.

> AIDEN
> What is crybaby doing up here?

> CAL
> Aiden, you did all of this?

> AIDEN
> (laughs)
> What do you mean?

> CAL
> You killed Nora, didn't you?

AIDEN becomes solemn.

> AIDEN
> What do you mean? Nora's not dead, you fool.

> CAL
> (angrily)
> Stop lying, Aiden.

                              AIDEN
              Woah, what are you getting angry for? I did
              nothing. Can't you just leave me alone?

                              CAL
                            (yelling)
              I know you did it, Aiden.

                              AIDEN
                            (yelling)
              Did what? Kill her? You can't be serious.

CAL pushes AIDEN and AIDEN pushes CAL back. Out of rage, CAL throws a
fist into AIDEN's face and he turns, with blood spewing from his nose.
                         AIDEN (CONT'D)
              Oh, you want to fight, huh?

AIDEN jabs CAL in the stomach and CAL falls back. AIDEN approaches CAL.

                         AIDEN (CONT'D)
              Too weak to fight back? That's what I thought.

CAL springs up and tackles Aiden. Both of them collide on the floor. On top of
AIDEN, CAL lifts up his arm up and smacks AIDEN countless times. AIDEN
does not get a single second to hit back. AIDEN lies, almost unconscious.

CAL pulls AIDEN up by gripping AIDEN's shirt and slams AIDEN's head to
the rails. Now on the floor, AIDEN does not move as blood drips from his
wound.

                            A VOICE
              You have failed. Please try again.

                                                    DISSOLVE TO:

INT. A PHYSICS CLASSROOM - 8:00 AM, TUESDAY

The classroom is empty. MR. MORLEY is at his desk, reading the newspaper.
CAL, dismayed, sits down at his seat with his head on the desk. He has gotten so
far, but at the same time, nowhere.

CAL stares down at his ongoing stopwatch. It reads 36:00:00.

                               247

CAL (V.O.)

36 hours.

MR. MORLEY flips a page.

CAL (V.O.)
I've been at this for 36 hours.

We get a close up shot of the Newton's cradle at work.

CAL (V.O.)
Nora's dead, isn't she? After all of
my attempts, she truly is dead.

We get a close up shot of Newton's pendulum ball turning.

CAL (V.O.)
Why is this happening to me? Why am I
suffering?

MR. MORLEY looks up from his newspaper and notices CAL.

MR. MORLEY
Cal! You're awake!

CAL

What's going on?

MR. MORLEY
The students are working on a lab on the roof.
We're measuring the speed of an object due to
air resistance. Mr. Gonzalez and Mrs. Zhang
are up there as well. Please come with me.

CUT TO:

EXT. THE SCHOOL'S ROOF - LATER
CAL pushes the door open and finds himself alone at the rooftop. He has a
feeling of deja-vu. He wonders where the students are.

CAL
(turning around)
Mr. Morley, you said there was a lab -

Silence.

248

As CAL turns around, he finds himself held at gunpoint. MR. MORLEY grips the 187 mm glock at CAL's face.

MR. MORLEY
You think you can get away so easily, Cal?

CAL
It was you the whole time?

Without moving the gun, MR. MORLEY jerks his head up and cackles.

MR. MORLEY
That's correct, Cal. All of those text messages. All of Nora's deaths. That was all of my doing.

CAL
But why … why did you put me through all of this?

MR. MORLEY
(sighs)
For decades, I've perfected the art of time loops and reality leaping. I knew that someday, someone out there will ruin my plans. That person is your sister, Nora.

CAL
Nora knew all of this?

MR. MORLEY
She did. She was my brightest student! That little brat wanted to know everything about physics, so I taught her everything. She had aspirations in time travel and time loops. What a silly girl! But the brat knew too much, which was why I had tried to murder her on a couple of occasions. She wanted to ruin my reputation and fame. I didn't want that to happen. She wanted to tell everyone my secret. She wanted to tell you first. You see, I wanted you to suffer. It was the only way to retaliate.

But now, once the secret's out, I guess it's
time for me to put you out of this temporal
misery. Goodnight, Cal.

Mr. Morley is about to pull the trigger. A sound of a gun being fired is heard. CAL
closes his eyes and pulls up his arms to defend himself.

Silence.

CAL opens his eyes and finds out he has not been shot. He glances at MR.
MORLEY, who stands still, petrified. A patch of blood leaks out of his left side.

MR. MORLEY howls and falls to the ground in knee position. Behind him, a
panting NORA holds a pistol. MR. MORLEY throws an agitated glare at NORA.

                         MR. MORLEY
                          (angrily)
              How did you …

                           NORA
              Mr. Morley, I know the truth.

NORA points the gun at MR. MORLEY. A river of tears stream down MR.
MORLEY's face.

                         MR. MORLEY
              Please, don't do this, Nora…Remember the
              times we had together? You were the best
              student I've ever had in my entire life!

                           NORA
                    (her face turns dark)
              I've been through all those deaths because of
              you. And I can never be more grateful to
              see you die in front of me.

NORA pulls the trigger and MR. MORLEY's body falls to the ground.

NORA approaches CAL and pulls her arms around him.

                           CAL
              Nora …

                            250

                              NORA
              I saw your text messages, Cal.

                              CAL
              Even if they were from a different reality?

                              NORA
              Yeah. It appears that I still get the same
              messages even in different time loops.

CAL and NORA head to the railings at the edge of the building's roof. They gaze
down at the city before them.

                              CAL
              So what do we do now?

                              NORA
                     (smiles into the distance)
              I don't know, Cal. I've been dead for so
              long, it's hard to adjust to living.

                              CAL
                          (laughs)
              Oh, come on, Nora…stop messing with me.

CAL stares longingly at NORA. Her hair flows like waves in the air. We get a
close-up shot of NORA's hair taking in the breeze.

                           CAL (V.O.)
              The Nora that stands in front of me doesn't
              remind me of the old Nora I once knew. It's
              odd. Maybe it's deja-vu or something. I just
              can't put my finger on it. Maybe this
              isn't Nora at all.

NORA laughs maniacally while CAL laughs sheepishly with her. The same
distorted music from the very beginning plays. We are left in the dark, lost in an
unfamiliar reality forever.

                                                          FADE OUT.

THE TURTLE DOVE'S SONG

By Kimberly Nguyen

Upon leaving home, I heard a familiar sound:
The gentle coos of your favorite bird echoing through the sky.
I remember you telling me how special those calls were,
Bringing back those precious, long-gone memories of the past.
The song, as quiet as it may be, brought a sense of comfort.
It was the beautiful coos of the turtle doves' song.

I, a child, looking to the sky
Searching, wondering, questioning where the clouds were.
You take me by the hand, humming your favorite song
Only pausing to tell me to listen to the turtle dove's gentle sound.
It was the doves' song for children, to bring them comfort
On the darkest of days, a message that the danger was now past.

Closing my eyes, I listened to the birds' quiet but beautiful song.
Your aged hand's protective grip filled me with an unbreakable comfort,
As if you, yourself, carried the warmth and kindness of that gentle sound.
You, those feelings, and that warmth are now only a part of the past.
Now here I stand, searching, wondering, questioning the sky.
Hoping the turtle doves' song returns things to how they once were.

On that particular morning, I was in need of that same feeling of comfort,
As my mind had been ravishing the troubling events of the past.
It wasn't until I had lifted my head to the morning sky
That I was met with the peace that came from the turtle doves' song.
I turned my head to the branch where the doves were,
Taking in that familiar yet consoling sound.

It was as if you had come happily visiting from the distant past,
Picking up where we had left off, exactly how we were.
All my troubles were lifted by the turtle doves' tuneful song.
Replacing my stress and worries with the memories of comfort,
I remembered your favorite song and your voice's mellow sound.
Like the birds' song, yours too echoed through the sky.

Now every morning, I search the sky to see where the birds were,
I wait outside the house, before leaving, awaiting that same routine sound.
Through the morning mist, my eyes scan the newly awakened sky,
For it is on the coldest of days that the turtle dove's song,
Rings the clearest, as it did on that one special day in our past.
It is out of the silence of the dawn that the gentle coos bring the most comfort.

As you make yourself comfortable with the other stars in the sky,
We who remain here on Earth treasure our memories now past,
Listening to the turtle doves' song, cherishing as if you were here.

A MESSAGE
By Kristy Diep

Sometimes I snooze so much that
I'll neglect the small possibility that
Someone might need my help today
That someone might need an answer
That I do not have, but can help them
Get to.

I tuck myself away because
I am ashamed to be in a world
Where issues on stage are unnoticed
Until someone pulls back the curtains
To reveal something that has
Always been there.

You see
We all grieve and suffer from
Loss
Despite it being mine
Or yours, or neither of ours
It's something that's shared.

We carry on
Though we feel the pain
We see the tears
We send our condolences
And try to understand.

Through a screen
We are all walking with our heads
Low
We are behind trending hashtags
Meme pages
And virtual personalities

We were taught to be
Nice since kindergarten
So we don't need authority
To tell us that our minds
Are spiralling bullets waiting
To be stopped
No
We cannot be silenced.

DONNA TRAN
By Peter Vu

I taped down both of my eyelids,
Because I didn't want to see a day without you.
Though I still see your pretty face,
But it must be a part of my hallucinations.

My fragile heart is all for you,
Because yours is underneath and not beating at all.
I miss you and love you so much,
But I can't tell you because you're not here anymore.

I hate when I'm alone at night,
Because I start and I won't stop crying over you.
I hoped for you to meet my kids,
But you'll be busy painting the oceans and skies blue.

Visiting you makes me happy,
Because I can feel your presence every time I come.
I sit near you and talk to you,
But I don't know if you're really there, can you hear me?

HELP ME

By Katia Navarrete

Please, someone help me!
Anyone!
Don't leave me alone.
My monsters, my fears, my doubts.
They come to haunt me when I'm alone.
I can't handle it!
My monsters creep behind me like a panther stalking prey.
They latch onto me when I'm raveled into my own self-doubts.
Their claws grab onto my soul, where they'll know every single thing
about me.
My breathing becomes uneven like the edge of a broken glass shard.
Someone help me! I can't breathe!
I don't want to be here anymore!
Every day I become more like the smoke.
My soul deteriorating from constant overthinking.
Someone, please help me!
I waited and waited until someone helped me, I begged for someone to
help me.
No one came, no sweet nothings, no 'it's going to be okay'
That's when I learned, not everyone can help me.
It's me, I have helped myself.

LOVE IS CRUEL

By Katia Navarette

You're going to be okay, he told me, I'm still going to be there for you.
No it's not going to be okay, I won't be able to tell him how much I love him
      every day.
Maybe I haven't told him enough times, maybe that's why he's leaving me.
Maybe I haven't gave him enough kisses, he might have forgotten how my lips feel
      against his.
Maybe that was why he left me.
It's not you, he said, it's me.
The most common phrase that has been used for years!
And he used it against me, against me!
I never knew he was this selfish,
I never knew he would actually use the oldest phrase in the book.
I wondered how many girls he used that phrase on to get out of the relationship
He started using my name instead of the pet names that he gave me.
Every time he said it, it was too much for me to handle.
I loved it when he said my name, but now my chest felt as if it was fragile glass
      with his voice banging into it repeatedly.
Maybe that was why he broke my heart into small glass shards with his sharpened
      words.
Maybe I wasn't as pretty as he said I was.
Maybe all the compliments that he told me were just lies that are still wrapped
      around my soul.
Maybe it wasn't meant to be.

FROM MY FINGERTIPS
By Thanhchau Chu

A harmonious melody springs from the tips of my fingers
With the notes of a lullaby and the sound of nature's wind
That puts to sleep my eyes and lays to rest my mind
For hours on end until the last key is played and heavy again is my heart
Wishing that the ringing in my ears would never go.
Do
Re
Mi
Fa
So
La
Ti
Do
One note bounces off the fingertips, the next wakes the ears
with a crash
Then it's time for the dance break
Hopping from one key
to the next
in a coordinated tune
Before the fingers landslide through the piano
for the last blow.

OVERLOAD

By Thanhchau Chu

What exactly is mental health?
Is it the number of vitamins you've taken?
Or the types of veggies you've ingested?
Is it the hours of exercise you've had?
Or the fact that you've actually stepped out to see the sun?
Is it not the time you've saved for yourself?
To relax and to enjoy the company of others?
Is it the amount of sleep you've gotten on weekends?
After a long week of assessments that never seem to stop?
Isn't it, in the end, the absence of Fridays scheduled for
One quiz, two tests, and two more essays followed by a presentation,
One after the other, back-to-back,
Like a set of punches that keep coming and coming?

The mental health the adults speak so fondly of
Is as far out of reach
As the planet Mars
Thanks to the overwhelming distance of expectations.
But once Mars is within reach,
Mental health will then be
Out of reach like the stars
Which will never be within hands' reach.

The world is overdosed on drugs
Keeping the cops busy all year round.
Well I'm, I'm overdosed on stress
And yet, I'm sitting here safe and sound.

Apparently stress is not that big of an issue
Seeing how educators, parents, and society
Are doing nothing to stop this student madness
From taking over and ruining our minds and our psych.

Drugs kill the brain
Manipulating it, degrading it
And stress is the same
But it just appears under a different name.

AUTHOR BIOS

Thanhchau Chu

Made in Vietnam, Thanh, whose real name is Chau, whose family name Chu is Chinese, is the middle child of triplet sisters born on the eve of the New Year. She loves boba and alleviates stress with kpop and kdrama.

Kristy Diep

Made with love, Kristy has always lived in Orange County, California. She wishes to travel around the world and not only write of her journey but photograph it as well. She aspires to make a difference and renew faith in humanity through her inspiring words, hoping that one day we'll achieve world peace.

Christine Do

Born in Southern California, Christine Do grew up in Garden Grove and developed a love for painting, drawing, and writing. She began to write her own stories in 4th grade. In the future she wishes to study business and English.

Jacqueline Hermosillo

Jacqueline, who goes by Jackie, grew up in Fountain Valley. In elementary school she developed a great love for Justin Bieber. She perfected the art of fangirling and indulged in buying makeup, eating poké, drinking coffee and writing. Jackie hopes to be a lawyer and to continue writing.

Jennifer T. Ho

Jennifer T. Ho was born in California, where, at a young age, she developed passion for the arts including painting and photography. In addition to art, she loves American football and pigs. She also goes by the nickname "Yennifer" and is an aspiring journalist.

Kelly Ho

Throughout her life, Kelly Ho has been involved in performing, drawing, and writing. Growing up in Southern California has exposed her to many cultures. The Vietnamese and Korean film industries, in particular, inspire much of her writing. "Dumb Love" is her first published work.

Nancy Huynh

Originally from Vietnam, Nancy Huynh grew up in Westminster where she became a music fanatic and self-proclaimed boba queen. She finds joy in learning new languages, exploring different cities, and writing poetry. Her supportive family inspires her to be lighthearted and optimistic.

Thanh Le

Throughout her childhood in Southern California, Thanh Le was immersed in the world of fiction. Video games, most notably Pokemon and Fire Emblem, inspire her to infuse her writing with adventure, fantasy, and nature.

Vy Le

Born in Vietnam, Vy Le came to the U.S only a year ago at the age of sixteen. She began her new life in Santa Ana where she has been discovering new things such as expressing her thoughts and feelings through her writing. She is on her way to make her dream become true—to become a doctor.

Katia Navarrete

Originally from California, Katia Navarrete grew up in the city of Garden Grove where she discovered her love of reading, writing and drawing. She began writing stories and poems in her early teen years in hopes to be published. Katia aspires to leave her mother's home and become a teacher.

Vy Ngo

Vy Ngo, originally from Vietnam, moved to America at the age of eight and now attends La Quinta High School. She is fluent in both Vietnamese and English. Her first publication was a children's story titled "Don't Worry, Younis, We're Here For You."

Aithy Nguyen

Growing up in a household who hates reading, Aithy Nguyen did not discover her passion for writing until she was accidentally enrolled in a creative writing class. A proud vegan, Aithy enjoys writing fiction, watching movies, and baking and cooking.

Alvin Nguyen

Alvin Nguyen, having grown up in California, values friends and family above all. He loves long thrilling adventures and enjoys writing poetry and stories. "Family" was his first published poem and the following year, "Family V2" was published. Alvin is studying to become an engineer.

Derek Nguyen

Born in Thousand Oaks and raised in Westminster, Derek Nguyen enjoys listening to most types of music, watching Star Wars movies, and taking naps. He writes mostly science fiction and action, but hopes to expand to other genres. He plans to study medicine to become a pharmacist or medical researcher.

HongAnh Nguyen

Hardworking and ambitious, young writer HongAnh Nguyen loves writing short stories but had found a passion for poetry since she joined creative writing. Despite her love for English literature, HongAnh hopes to major in social science or biotechnology in the near future.

Johnson Nguyen

Born in California, Johnson Nguyen moved to New Mexico before returning to California at the age of four. He developed an interest in football during middle school and didn't write much until he took creative writing in high school. He would like to be a pharmacist in the future.

Kimberly Nguyen

Cheerful, caring, and a bit clumsy, Kimberly Nguyen enjoys hanging out with friends, spending time with her family, and binge watching her favorite shows. Previously published in "Train of Thoughts", she hopes to continue to publish her poetry and stories and pursue a career working with animals.

Kristen Nguyen

Born in Westminster, California, Kristen Nguyen is a strong, passionate, and cheerful soul who always has a smile on her face. She enjoys reading, writing, and music, and of course, hanging out with friends and family. "Demons Disguised As Soldiers" is her first published poem.

Michelle Nguyen

Michelle Nguyen was born in Fountain Valley where she discovered a love for tennis, acoustic guitar, and dogs. In her free time, she doodles and writes in her journal. One day, she aspires to become a pediatrician and decorate her office with pictures of her and her family from their many trips together.

Thanh Nguyen

Thanh Nguyen (Thannie) is from Southern California. She is a creative young woman with a passion for new adventures. Her life revolves around League of Legends, motorcycles, and music. When it comes to short stories, she loves to write about romance.

Kelvin Pham

Rabid frequenter of Shrek the Musical and Avenue Q, Kelvin Pham lives in Westminster where he developed a profound interest in musicals, drawing, mock trial, and writing screenplays. As a result of watching an obscene amount of the Sci-Fi Channel, his first published screenplay is "Reality Leap."

Hien Phan

Self-proclaimed hope advocate HienPhan writes to remind themselves and everyone around them that there is such thing as beauty in the world. While chronic screaming is their hobby, they can be seen writing song lyrics or playing games about archers and cyborg ninjas.

Krista Phanpraphou

From Southern California, Krista Phanpraphou wakes up every morning with a daily dose of Vietnamese coffee. Her first written work--an unreadable love letter for a golden retriever. She wants to learn Swedish, study at Stockholm University, and become a veterinarian or criminologist.

Karen Phung

Growing up, Karen Phung always filled her life with aspirations, such as her current one—to go zip-lining. She's developed interests in drawing, writing, and graphic design. She's clueless of what to do in the future, but in the meantime, she writes poems to express her perceptions on life.

Edison Sesmas

Raised in the clement SoCal city of Westminster, Edison was born into a mestizo-American family. At home, he enjoys studying both U.S. and European history as a pastime. Being a superb scholar, Edison aspires to attend U.C.I. and launch his career in the medical field.

Daniela Solano

Born in California into a reserved household, Daniela Solano lives her "double life" by expressing herself through her various passions, which include writing, music, dancing. She one day hopes to be an example for people that feel trapped within the constraints of society/family, unable to convey their creativity.

Alyssa Starnes

Ever since she was young, Alyssa moved in and out of foster care homes because of family problems. Now back with her family in Westminster, she has overcome tremendous obstacles to become the first in her family to graduate high school. She enjoys photography and plans to teach it in the future.

Vivian Tang

Vivian Tang lives in Westminster, California. As a unique and charismatic teenager, Vivian draws in individuals with her bubbly personality and contagious laughter. She is passionate about watercolor painting, tear-jerking dramas, and Frappuccino's with the perfect amount of whipped cream.

Phuong Traceyle

Originally from Garden Grove, Phuong Traceyle lives in Westminster. She is energetic, funny, and kind to her friends and family. She loves bubble tea and playing sports with her cousins. Although she does not like to read novels, she enjoys creating short stories.

Clarisse Tran

Born into a family that emigrated from Vietnam, Clarisse Tran learned the value of education, hard work, and self-expression. Her favorite self-expression is writing. As a young child, she discovered a love for composing poems. She plans to go into the medical field and express her creativity through writing.

Emily Tran

Emily Tran, born in Fountain Valley, California, attends La Quinta High School and aspires to help people in any way possible. Her love for books and music inspire her to write stories and poems with an aim to make people happy.

Vylan Tran

Vylan Tran was born and raised in Fountain Valley, California. She likes romantic novels and would someday like to make some. Her first published poem "She" is in the book "Train of Thoughts." She aspires to make a positive difference in the world.

April Trinh

April Trinh is a clumsy individual who suffers from bad luck. She finds that she can either master something, like coding, in one try or spend the rest of her life not even knowing the half of it. She enjoys graphic design and computer science, and speaks English, Vietnamese, Java, and screaming.

Tony Truong

Born in California, Tony Truong was raised in Westminster by his single mother along with his brother and sister. Tony enjoys long walks on the beach, playing with dogs, and reading young adult novels. Although he rarely gets along with teachers, Tony aspires to become one after finishing school.

Peter Vu

Born in Fountain Valley, Peter Vu grew up along the border between Westminster and Garden Grove. He fell in love with film and writing. Most of his writings are private, except "Don't Forget Charlie," which was his first published poem (Train of Thoughts). He aspires to write and create films.

Monson Wilson

Originally from California, Monson grew up in Rialto where he developed a passion to play flag football. Practicing hard on the field, he, along with his La Quinta High School team, made it to the CIF Championship this year. This is his first publication.

www.ingramcontent.com/pod-product-compliance
Lightning Source LLC
Chambersburg PA
CBHW060906250626
47159CB00008B/2892